insight series

An insight into
Anxiety

Copyright © Waverley Abbey Trust 2023
Published 2023 by Waverley Abbey Trust, Waverley Abbey House, Waverley Lane, Farnham, Surrey GU9 8EP, UK. Registered Charity No. 294387. Registered limited company No. 1990308. Previously published by CWR in 2007.
The rights of Chris Ledger and Clare Blake to be identified as the authors of this work have been asserted by them in accordance with the Copyright, Designs and Patents Act 1988, sections 77 and 78.
All rights reserved. No part of this publication may be reproduced, stored in a retrieval system, or transmitted, in any form or by any means, electronic, mechanical, photocopying, recording or otherwise, without the prior permission in writing of Waverley Abbey Trust.
For a list of National Distributors, visit waverleyabbeytrust.org/distributors
Unless otherwise indicated, all Scripture references are from the *NIV*, New International Version® Anglicised, NIV® Copyright © 1979, 1984, 2011 by Biblica, Inc.® Used by permission. All rights reserved worldwide. Other translations: *NRSV*, New Revised Standard Version Bible: Anglicized Edition, Copyright © 1989, 1995 by National Council of the Churches of Christ in the United States of America. Used by permission. All rights reserved worldwide; *Phillips* Modern English Bible, by J. B. Phillips, "The New Testament in Modern English", Copyright© 1962 by HarperCollins; *The Message* copyright © 1993, 2002, 2018 by Eugene H. Peterson. Used by permission of NavPress. All rights reserved. Represented by Tyndale House Publishers, Inc.

Every effort has been made to ensure that this book contains the correct permissions and references, but if anything has been inadvertently overlooked, the Publisher will be pleased to make the necessary arrangements at the first opportunity. Please contact the Publisher directly.
Concept development and editing by Waverley Abbey Trust.
Design and typesetting by Clare James
Cover image: Adobe Stock/Kryuchka Yaroslav
Printed and bound in the UK.
Paperback ISBN: 978-1-78951-489-6
eBook ISBN: 978-1-78951-490-2

About the authors

CHRIS LEDGER worked as a counsellor, supervisor and trainer in the NHS, and now has a private practice. She enjoys speaking at Christian meetings and is a regular tutor at Waverley Abbey Resources' Insight Days, also co-authoring several books in this series. She is a licensed lay minister at Greyfriars Church, Reading.

CLARE BLAKE is a Christian author and journalist with a passion for seeing Christian women grow in God. Mother of two grown-up sons and grandmother to several grandchildren, Clare lives with her husband in Bristol, where they attend City Church, sharing its vision for reaching out to the surrounding community.

DR LYNN SUTER is a psychologist who has worked in the NHS and private practice, as well as having been a clinical director for a Christian counselling agency. She has also taught on the Masters programmes at Waverley Abbey College and been a supervisor for a Christian counselling agency in the West Midlands where she now lives.

insight
series

The *Waverley Abbey Insight Series* has been developed in response to the great need to help people understand and face some key issues that many of us struggle with today. In these books, there are insights that will help you gain a deeper knowledge about these challenges and how they can impact us emotionally, spiritually and physically. They draw from the Waverley Integrative Framework which gives an accessible map for understanding how problems can affect us. The writers also offer some practical and sensitive skills to navigating the issues, based firmly on a Christian perspective. The resources in this series are both thorough and succinct, written by authors with extensive experience and knowledge. Whether you are in a helping role or struggling in your own life, it is our prayer that these books will support and bless you, bringing you deeper into the knowledge of the Lord who heals.

WAVERLEY ABBEY
TRUST

Contents

Foreword – Lady Eileen Carey	6
Introduction	8
1. What is Anxiety?	11
2. Who is Vulnerable to Anxiety?	21
3. How Anxiety Affects Us	37
4. Understanding Specific Anxieties	53
5. Skills to Help Overcome Anxiety	75
Appendices	100
Endnotes	106
Further reading	107

Foreword

If I were asked to describe modern society with one word, I could think of no better one than 'anxious'. We live in an 'anxious society' and so many lives are dominated by fear – fear of crime, of terrorism, of intrusion, of global warming and climate change, of asylum seekers and so on. And, in fact, every institution in society seems to be afflicted by a general climate of anxiety, including the Church. Christians fear decline, we fear growth, and we fear change.

In our individual lives there is so much overwork, stress and busyness that it's little wonder that we learn to experience fear and anxiety over apparently minor things. We are so concerned about image that even as we go about leisure activities we are bothered about how we look to others. In their careers, so many people are overburdened with expectations that they find it difficult to balance work with home life.

Even the pleasures of a family life are infected by varying degrees of panic about whether the children will get into the right school or get the right exam results. In fact, facing the pressure of tests and exams, our children and grandchildren are being exposed to anxiety and fear of failure at an earlier age than ever before.

Healthy fear teaches caution in the face of danger. Unhealthy anxiety can paralyse us and destroy lives.

It is little wonder then that so many people experience the symptoms of anxiety in both mild and extreme forms, including panic attacks, phobias, social anxiety and generalised anxiety disorder.

Chris Ledger, Clare Blake and Lynn Suter have provided yet another excellent introduction into a contemporary problem in the *Waverley Abbey Insight Series* with *An insight into Anxiety*. Chris writes from her extensive experience as a counsellor, a Christian lay minister and a long-term carer for her daughter, Julia, who suffers from ME.

Consequently, this is not merely a clinical introduction to anxiety, nor a theoretical one, but a deeply practical and helpful overview of the subject. As well as providing a must-read account of the nature of anxiety, psychological understandings of the term, and descriptions of how it is experienced by so many people today, the book offers very helpful steps for overcoming different symptoms of anxiety, including relaxation and breathing exercises, as well as more fundamental pointers towards reorientating one's life and learning to be at ease.

There are also theological insights aplenty as the authors identify a number of biblical texts that deal with anxiety. The key lesson for the contemporary Christian is to remember that while the Bible admonishes us not to be anxious, this is not to make us feel even worse about ourselves. The point is that by casting our anxiety upon God we find security and refuge from even our deepest fears. This is a spiritual discipline which Clare, Chris and Lynn ably combine with the practice of counselling.

Lady Eileen Carey

Introduction

NOTE FROM JANET PENNY, Insight Series Editor
To be anxious is to be human; we have been adeptly made with an internal system that warns us of threat and primes us for action in the face of challenges. This bodily 'flight, fight or freeze' response serves us well in the heat of the moment. But, as many of us know, pressures and difficulties can leave us with too much anxiety that can linger and overwhelm. How then, as a Christian, in the light of God's encouragement to know His peace, can we navigate a path towards managing anxiety? This book provides a thorough and practical introduction to understanding anxiety with a biblical perspective in mind. It gives clear information on some of the main aspects of what anxiety is and practical strategies for finding relief. At the end of the chapters, you are invited to pause, reflect and pray - an invitation to know the Lord's presence with us, even in our anxiety. Whether you are helping someone suffering with anxiety or struggling yourself, this insight into anxiety is a good starting place to explore a healing path, and my prayer is that it will lead you deeper into God's peace.

NOTE FROM CLARE BLAKE
This book has grown out of a seminar given by Chris Ledger at Waverley Abbey House and demonstrates Chris's deep concern for those whose lives are blighted by anxious feelings. Anxiety affects many people, whether mildly, with a tendency to worry, or severely, when it can seriously affect the quality of life of the person suffering. The book explores the subject in depth, seeking to help us understand exactly what anxiety is, what causes it, and how we can manage our anxiety with the help of proven skills and strategies.

In these pages Chris draws on a rich fund of wisdom gained from her work as an experienced counsellor, her role as a licensed lay minister, and particularly her own very personal experience as a long-term carer for her daughter with ME, where Chris learned to hand her anxiety over to a loving God who, she discovered, was faithful in every circumstance.

> Cast all your anxiety on him because he cares for you.
> **1 PETER 5:7**

NOTE FROM CHRIS LEDGER

Worry, fear and anxiety can be like psychological poisons causing great distress, as in releasing their deadly toxins they appear to contaminate our whole being. However, there are antidotes. The first is to find a greater security in our heavenly Father so that we can go to Him with childlike faith and trust Him with difficulties that are beyond our control. Secondly, we can actually learn how to manage the restricting mental, behavioural and bodily symptoms of the anxiety response which can be so very distressing and frightening for sufferers. In many years of counselling experience, I have found working with very anxious clients one of the most rewarding areas because lives can be so tangibly changed.

The purpose of this book is to help you put your roots deeper into the soil of God's love, thus becoming more dependent upon Him, and to give you the skills to manage and control the distressing symptoms of anxiety – not only for yourself, but also as you try to understand and help others. Clare and Lynn have done a fine job in taking my notes and creating a resourceful book which I hope and pray you will find helpful.

NOTE FROM DR LYNN SUTER

For some time *An insight into Anxiety* has been an amazing resource to help both anxiety sufferers and those supporting them. Having said that, research and knowledge about psychological conditions is being added to all the time. In this updated book we have tried to keep rooted in the Father's love and goodness whilst adding information based on more recent psychological and neuro-scientific knowledge. My hope is that these additions will help to add to your understanding about how anxiety works and how to manage it. More importantly I hope that having this knowledge will enable you also to be kind to yourself in the same way that God is kind to you.

Chapter 1
What is Anxiety?

A thin stream of fear trickling through the mind. If encouraged, it cuts a channel into which all other thoughts are drained.
ARTHUR SOMERS ROCHE[1]

What words or pictures spring to mind when you hear the term 'anxiety'? Delegates at one of Chris' conferences came up with some striking images:

Lots of twisted strands
A coiled string getting tighter
A furrowed brow
Running away
A quivering jelly
Out of control
Overwhelmed
Cast adrift
Tense
Help!

Vulnerable
Hopeless
Insecure
Wound up

The *Compact Oxford English Dictionary* tells us that anxiety is 'a concern about an imminent or future difficulty'[2] while the *Collins English Dictionary* describes it as 'distress of mind, apprehension, uneasiness, disquietude'.[3] Anxiety affects everyday living, bringing with it feelings of fear or panic that affect us physically and emotionally. Another particularly accurate description that Chris once heard is that anxiety is 'fear spread out thinly'.

Anxiety is rather like an octopus that enfolds us in a suffocating grasp that can be very hard to break. It includes distressing conditions such as phobias, social anxiety and panic attacks. Anxiety can impact both our physical and mental wellbeing, possibly causing heart trouble, high blood pressure, stomach disorders, irritable bowel syndrome, back and neck pain, migraine, headaches, fatigue, insomnia, depression, and many other conditions.

However, the good news is that anxiety can improve with the help of specific skills and strategies, and we can be comforted in our anxiety by placing our reliance on God. Anxious people can emerge from their distressing symptoms as they learn to manage their anxiety, rather than let their anxiety manage them.

Anxiety is a normal response

The first thing we must recognise is that anxiety is a normal part of the human experience. It is how God has made us, a natural response to what is going on around us, and healthy levels of anxiety are vital for our survival. It is the body's way of saying *Pay attention to this – it could have consequences for you.*

Anxiety is very much a part of daily life. For example, a person just about to go on stage may complain of 'stage fright' or performance anxiety. This is actually not a handicap but a benefit, as 'stage fright' releases extra adrenalin into the system, enabling an energy-charged performance. Another example is a person just about to take an exam whose anxiety 'gears up' the body for the approaching task. Anxiety is also an essential response to an imminent or future difficulty or threat.

When anxiety becomes a problem

However, anxiety becomes a problem when it is exaggerated, unmanageable or experienced out of context. In this scenario, anxiety may cause us not to think as clearly as usual, and a cycle of distress may develop.

For example, if you were about to cross a road in front of a bus, a certain amount of normal anxiety would ensure that you didn't get knocked down by it! However, if you were sitting in a park near a main road, and the presence of nearby buses made your anxiety levels rise steeply – *Oh my goodness, there are buses there.* – that could be very unmanageable.

While a normal and healthy anxiety response protects us, unhealthy anxiety is an exaggerated response, and can cause cycles of distress to develop. Levels of anxiety can be thought of as on a continuum, as demonstrated on page 14, where, at one end, the feelings we experience can be unmanageable and are focused on a perceived threat, or are not a proportional response to a situation.

A continuum for healthy and unhealthy anxiety

Healthy anxiety (the right response to a real threat – eg *If I met a lion, I would run for my life.*)

Unhealthy anxiety (an out-of-balance response – eg *I avoid flying because I am terrified the plane will crash.*)

What is anxiety?

Many people confuse anxiety with stress, but where the latter is more to do with our reactions to pressure, anxiety is a response to any issue we encounter that provokes a sense of fear within us. Anxiety raises questions such as:

- Will I cope?
- Am I adequate?
- What will happen?
- Will it work out OK?

In its simplest form, anxiety is a fear response to a perceived threat. The first issue when trying to help a person with any anxiety problem is to help them to explore what they perceive their threat is and to consider the likelihood of what they predict will happen actually happening.

For instance, a woman could be facing a physical threat because her partner is an alcoholic who is sometimes abusive. This is a real threat and her fear relating to possible violence is an appropriate anxiety. However, the anxiety could also be triggered by an imagined threat. The woman this time may be in a relationship with a new partner who has never been drunk or violent towards her. The woman may still feel anxious about being abused by her partner even though the evidence is that he would not touch her. In this instance the woman's anxiety, whilst understandable given her previous experience, is based on an unfounded fear.

The fear, however, whether well-founded or not, feels very real to the person, and their anxiety levels may soar. Anxiety then becomes a problem if the person feels unable to find a solution for their situation. It can become an ongoing condition in which the person nearly always feels fearful. This in turn can severely limit a person's life as, at its worst, they can be afraid even to get out of bed. People with anxiety often expect the worst to happen and predict that it will. For example, the anxiety that comes from having experienced unwanted and inappropriate comments from others can lead someone to predict that if they go out they will experience this again, so it is best to stay in the house, if not in bed.

Anxiety feelings

Anxiety can take many forms. Often the feelings involve:
- a deep uncertainty about the future with an accompanying feeling of dread
- questions such as: *What will happen?, Will I be able to cope?*
- an overwhelming sense of panic that something awful is about to happen
- an inner sense of being inadequate, which can lead to a sense of shame (this is often the case in social anxiety)
- a very real sense of being worried about almost anything (generalised anxiety disorder (GAD)
- very specific fear (phobia).

Anxiety can be an immensely strong feeling. Have you ever

experienced high levels of anxiety as you really, really hoped that you would not be the one chosen for something that you didn't want to do? In such a situation your heart thumps as though it is going to explode, your body feels very tense, and maybe your palms get hot and sweaty. *Anybody else please – just not me!* These bodily symptoms are caused by anxiety.

There are things that happen physiologically when we are anxious commonly known as the 'fight or flight' (or freeze) response. In this state the autonomic nervous system kicks in and makes the body ready to fight or to flee the perceived threat. Often we are not able to actually fight, so fleeing by withdrawing is a common response in people with anxiety.

Anxiety and the Waverley Integrative Framework

However, anxiety affects far more than just the physical area, as we will see if we look at the Waverley Integrative Framework (WIF), which illustrates the five areas that our anxiety may affect.

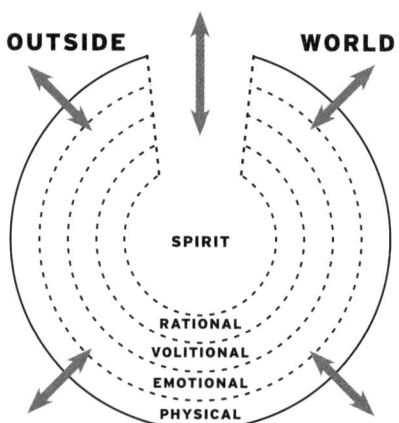

God created us as whole beings with every area interconnecting, and anxiety affects each area in different yet related ways.

- Physical – experiencing bodily symptoms of anxiety

- Rational – having generally unhelpful thoughts, causing psychological changes
- Emotional – experiencing emotions such as worry, apprehension, fear, anticipation
- Volitional – choosing to avoid or increase anxiety
- Spiritual – experiencing the effects of anxiety on personal faith

Anxiety impacts the physical area by causing symptoms in our body such as shortness of breath, tension, sweaty palms and others, while in the emotional area we may experience a wide variety of emotions in addition to the anxiety, including confusion and feeling out of control.

Anxiety affects our rational or thinking level where our thoughts can actually make the anxiety more overwhelming and more intense. For example, if you were to stand up to speak in front of an audience and think *I can't cope with this – they are all looking at me. I know I will run out of words and do a terrible job. This is awful. Why on earth am I here? What if they don't like me?* it is very likely that your anxiety would steadily rise.

On average we speak around 500 words a minute, but the self-talk going on in the subconscious mind averages a staggering 1,500 words a minute. So, if we feed our minds with negative thoughts such as *I can't cope. This is awful,* it is highly likely that we will end up feeling more anxious.

Another area affected by anxiety is our actual behaviour represented in the diagram by the volitional level. One of the most important factors in anxiety, and the reason that it often continues to be a problem, is that the common response to anxiety is to avoid the situation which creates it. Sadly, such avoidance nurtures the anxiety rather than dealing with it because, by avoiding the situation, we never find out that our predicted outcome, which causes our fear, very often does not come to pass.

And of course, importantly, we need to evaluate how well we are meeting our deep spiritual needs in God in the presence of anxiety. Research Research by Plante and Sherman into religious coping shows that faith can be both positively and negatively impacted by anxiety[4]. If anxiety is impacting us negatively, it is important for our wholeness that we learn to anchor ourselves in God.

An alternative anxiety model

Another useful way to identify how anxiety affects us is to write the word 'anxiety' in the middle of a piece of paper, and then write down how it affects the different areas of our life, as illustrated in the diagram below.

For example, symptoms might include hyper-vigilance, where a person simply can't shut their thoughts off so that their anxiety runs round and round in their head like a hamster in a wheel, or poor concentration, where the sufferer spends so much time trying to deal with the anxiety that it is impossible to focus on anything else.

You may find it helpful to explore your own individual experience of anxiety in this way, as it may help you to view it from a different perspective.

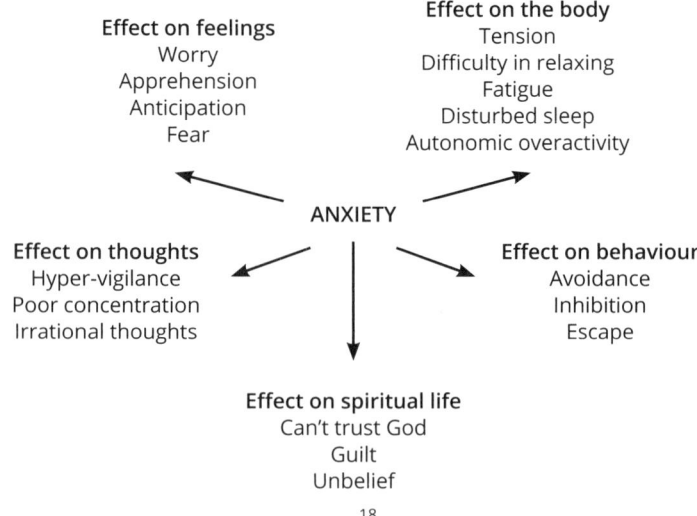

Activity

Think of a situation or an event that has given you a high level of anxiety, and use either the Waverley Integrative Framework on page 16 or the alternative anxiety model on page 18 to look at it from an objective perspective, examining what you experienced in the different areas. Ask yourself questions such as: *What were my thoughts at this point? How did anxiety affect my behaviour?*

Think carefully, explore your anxiety, and see where it produced the greatest effect, writing in as much detail as you can.

My event _____ (eg going to meet new people)

_____

_____

How do you feel when you see this information set out on paper? Does it help you see the big picture? This is a really helpful technique as it is not only releasing for the person with the anxiety, but is also a very constructive tool for those trying to help others. They can then identify specific issues by looking at what has been revealed, and ask *What's going on here? What areas need addressing?*

Reflection

Focus on the following verses:

> You who live in the shelter of the Most High,
>   who abide in the shadow of the Almighty,
> will say to the Lord, 'My refuge and my fortress;
>   my God, in whom I trust.'…
> Those who love me, I will deliver;
>   I will protect those who know my name.
> When they call to me, I will answer them;

> I will be with them in trouble,
> I will rescue them and honour them.

PSALM 91:1–2,14–15, NRSV

- Think about what it means to live 'in the shelter of the Most High'. How does that make you feel?
- Meditate for a few minutes on these words: refuge, fortress, rescue.
- How does the Lord respond when we are in trouble? What sort of things does He do?
- Think of a time or times when God has been a refuge to you. If you cannot personally remember such a time, look at the Bible for inspiration, eg Ruth, David, Joseph, or the lives of Christian pioneers such as Hudson Taylor and Mother Teresa.

Prayer

Father God, sometimes I just need to know that You are here for me. Thank You that I know that when I call to You, You are never too busy to hear me, and that You always respond. It helps me feel stronger just to know that You promise to be with me whatever happens if I call on Your name. Thank You that even though I don't always understand some of the things that I am going through, I can hold on to the fact that You say that You will be with me – I couldn't wish for anything better.

Thank You that when I feel anxious and alone, You promise to provide a shelter for me where I can rest in You. Help me to really let that truth sink into me. Amen.

Chapter 2
Who is vulnerable to anxiety?

> Worry often gives a small thing a big shadow.
> ANON

Some people seem to be more vulnerable to feeling anxious than others, and significant life events may also deeply affect anxiety levels. Such events can be any sort of trauma where we have been emotionally, physically or sexually abused, or car accidents, terrorist experiences, illness or death, or things we are taught in childhood (eg *If you are naughty the police will take you away*), and challenging experiences, (eg giving a public talk, having a new baby, redundancy).

Personalities susceptible to anxiety

Research has shown that some types of personality are more susceptible to anxiety than others. Many anxiety sufferers have what psychologists describe as Type A personalities. This means that they are often viewed as extremely competitive, out-performing and self-critical. They tend to be driven and predisposed towards anxiety because their desire to achieve is nearly always partnered by a fear of failure. On the other hand, shy and withdrawn people may also often become anxious because they have never learnt to be assertive and fear rejection if they say 'no'.

A dysfunctional family

Another common factor is family history. Growing up in an atmosphere where negative messages pollute the home, or where a parent suffers with a generalised anxiety disorder (GAD) can leave a child thinking it is normal to be anxious.

Such an upbringing is rather like growing up in a fairground 'hall of mirrors'. Year after year you are presented with a distorted image of yourself with big head and little bowed legs, until finally you come to believe it. Not even a glimpse of yourself as you actually are in an ordinary mirror can convince you otherwise.

This is just what can happen to those unfortunate enough to grow up in a family where the message that they are 'no good' is constantly reflected back day after day. With the constant refrain *I am no good because I have been told I'm no good. I can't do this. I can't possibly do that* troubling their mind, it is no wonder that they have problems with confidence and find anxiety levels hit the ceiling when asked to undertake a task such as speaking at a conference.

Other anxiety factors

Another factor in anxiety is a psychologically biased thinking style, as we will discover in the next chapter. Stressful circumstances also play a significant role, especially if several life stresses occur together, because anxiety is a common by-product of stress. The amount of anxiety we experience is also partly dependent on how well developed our coping skills are, again often linked to our personality type or family background. Another contributory factor is the presence or absence of a good social support system as, if we lack that vital network of family and friends, our anxiety levels often increase sharply.

Common sources of anxiety

There are many different issues that can cause us anxiety and these often vary according to our stage in life. For example, as we get older, health may become a major cause of anxiety, whereas for younger people lack of finance may head the list. The following list contains some of the most common anxiety factors, and obviously a combination of two or more may greatly increase anxiety levels, eg a husband losing his job and a wife becoming pregnant. It's interesting to note that even positive life events such as a longed-for marriage can add to our sense of stress and anxiety as we navigate changes in circumstances:

- Health
- Your children
- Your job
- Relationships
- Pregnancy
- Promotion
- Growing old
- Domestic upheaval
- Financial problems
- Legal difficulties
- Exams.

Identifying the threat

As already stated, anxiety is always a response to a perceived threat, and how high our anxiety rises depends on how strong we perceive that threat to be. There are three major types of anxiety based on three types of threat. The first one is the objective real threat, the second the subjective assessed threat, and the third is threats to expectations and self-image.

The objective real threat

The objective real threat is a very concrete form of threat. For instance, a firefighter must handle his fear of fire to perform his job properly. A personal example of an objective real threat was experienced when Chris's anxiety levels soared as never before during a trip to Florida.

The threat came from a surprising source, not the alligators in the Alligator Park where she and her husband were enjoying a relaxed picnic, but a squirrel that suddenly appeared beside their table, screaming and frothing at the mouth. Chris's immediate thought was rabies!

Her anxiety shot sky high – no way did she want to get rabies – and when the squirrel actually jumped onto the table, Chris didn't wait to see what would happen next, running away as fast as she could without even stopping to grab her lunch. In this case her anxiety was a valid response to a very objective real threat: the possibility that the squirrel might have rabies.

The subjective assessed threat (phobias)

However, the anxiety that prompted Chris's escape from this real threat might then have become distorted into anxiety caused by a subjective assessed threat (phobias). For instance, if she had a personality prone to anxiety, this experience might have prompted a continuing anxious response every time she saw a squirrel: *Rabies, I must run.*

This is the essence of the subjective assessed threat. We see a threat where there really is none and then the anxious thoughts can escalate to become phobias. A phobia (derived from a Greek word meaning fear or aversion) is considered to be an 'excessive fear' because no objective threat is involved.

In the case of phobias, anxiety levels rise steeply, and the nature of the response can be overwhelming and illogical, leading many people who have become phobic to think they are going crazy, whereas the real problem is simply that the phobia causes strange reactions in the body and in the mind.

Unfortunately, people who are phobic can find it very difficult to share what they are experiencing. They often feel ashamed because they actually recognise that their response is excessive, but it is nonetheless intensely real for them and causes great distress.

Threats to expectations and self-image

Threats to our expectations and self-image can come from a huge variety of sources. Anxiety can be caused by:

- possible promotion
- position in an academic class
- the fear of letting parents down
- a husband's lack of affection
- having a less smart home than friends/family
- trying to ask a girl for a date
- a lack of physical attraction
- the fear of making a fool of oneself in public
- making love (performance anxiety)
- visiting parents-in-law
- negotiating deals
- wondering what the neighbours think.

Anxiety can arise in these sorts of situations when we are concerned that we may fail our own or other people's expectations or high standards, or when our sense of self may be impacted.

Expectations and anxiety

However, if you look more closely at the list you will note that none of them actually poses an objective threat to survival. The threat that they pose is a threat to self-image, and this is the basis for many people's anxiety. They see a situation threatening a high level of expectation of themselves: the more important the expectation, the more serious the threat, and the greater the likelihood of anxiety.

Because such anxiety is a response to a perceived threat, it often triggers the 'fight or flight' mechanism which allows us to escape any situation that causes anxiety and might cast doubt on our self-image. However, this response generally maintains and strengthens our anxious feelings, causing strong emotional and physical reactions which can result in disturbances in our thinking, disturbances in our behaviour, and can ultimately affect our relationship with God.

> Layla, aged 34, was a late developer who had left school early without many qualifications. After working for a while she went to evening classes, studied hard, and got a place to study psychology at degree level. However, Layla was very aware of how much older she was than the other students. She felt boring and unattractive, and found it particularly hard when her limited computer skills caused considerable amusement amongst her fellow students.
>
> Although the degree was something that she really wanted to do, Layla found it harder and harder to go into the university as she was convinced that the lecturers and the other students all thought she was wasting her time. She was particularly anxious about the spoken presentations, and was beginning to suffer from a mild level of panic attack, which was growing increasingly stronger. She was constantly fatigued and kept crying at the least thing, which made her worry that she might be heading for a nervous breakdown.

Anxiety and our spiritual being

God has created us with deep spiritual needs: the need to feel a love tha gives us a sense of security; a love that brings self-worth;

and a love that gives us purpose in life. Anxiety may arise when these spiritual needs are not being met in a helpful way. In his book, Letters to Malcolm, C.S. Lewis describes anxiety as an 'affliction'.[1] This means it can just happen; it doesn't mean we have done something unhelpful or inappropriate. Anxiety can also often arise from a complicated interplay of factors, including personal disposition and situational factors. As we reflect on anxiety and spirituality, it can be helpful to hold in mind that causes of anxiety, and indeed other similar issues, are often complex and multifactorial. An activity can be helpful for wellbeing without the lack of it being the cause. In other words, growing closer to God can often help people with anxiety, but the cause of anxiety may be related to other factors apart from faith. As an example, exercise has been shown to help with symptoms of depression, but a lack of exercise is rarely the cause of depression. So, we can look to God knowing He will help, and does not condemn people for having anxiety.

> Jeremiah said, 'My people have committed two sins: They have forsaken me, the spring of living water, and have dug their own cisterns, broken cisterns that cannot hold water'
> JER. 2:13.

Jeremiah used the metaphor of broken cisterns to explain how Israel had abandoned Yahweh, the source of life and had substituted Him with other gods. We also often have broken cisterns because we worship other things in the place where God should be. This can sometimes mean that we try to meet spiritual needs through pursuing inappropriate goals. If we are not fully anchored in God then it is possible that when our goals become uncertain, anxiety can increase.

> Mark was very anxious because he was facing the

> uncertainty of his business folding. His goal had always been to have enough money to play and live well, and he now struggled to trust God for his future, because for him a future without money was bleak. He had not grown enough as a Christian to find his deep spiritual need for security met in God – he was digging a broken cistern. As a result, Mark felt very anxious about his future.

Of course, there is nothing wrong with a goal in itself. We all respond in one way or another to goals which we or others set. God Himself had a goal to create the earth and to rescue us from the penalty of sin through Jesus Christ.

However, goals can become a problem when they take over our lives, or if they are set in concrete and are not flexible enough. If we look at our goals instead of looking at God, we may quickly run into problems.

Activity
Do you relate to any of these thoughts/reflections on what might underlie anxiety?

Hidden goals

We all have hidden goals, which are goals that we find it hard to verbalise but that are important to us nonetheless.

In common with many people, Chris's hidden goal was the need to be accepted, a need rooted in her childhood where she grew up in the shadow of a dominant twin sister. Her sister was the lively one and got all the attention, so Chris's worth came to depend upon pleasing others in order to be accepted: *When I am accepted I am worth something. When people like me I feel better about myself.* Many of us have these sorts of messages that come from childhood, telling us that we have to do something in order to have worth. Thus we try to do those things, eg please people, try hard at everything, stay strong at all times, do things quickly etc.

Every hidden goal, such as needing to please people, raises issues that we need to confront directly by asking ourselves some important questions.

- Who am I trying to please?
- Why do I drive myself in this way?
- Do I behave like this to receive esteem?
- Do I want to be recognised?
- Does my hidden goal become a problem because I am neglecting my relationship with God?
- What is my motivation?
- What do I expect to get out of this?

Activity
What is your hidden goal? What do you strive for? Identifying this is often extremely illuminating and will help you to understand why you behave as you do. It may take time to uncover your hidden goals. If you are struggling to notice any, think about a time when you felt very anxious or upset and you felt as though there was something blocking your goal – what goal might you have been trying to reach? Ask the Holy Spirit to help you as you read and reflect. Write down your hidden goal to help clarify your thoughts.

_____

_____

Hidden beliefs

Similarly, we can also have hidden beliefs about ourselves that we may not even be conscious of, but nevertheless may be a powerful driving force beneath the surface.

For many people, their hidden beliefs have reinforced feelings of worthlessness: *I am no good. I am stupid. I am powerless.* Chris herself has found that when life gets difficult, her hidden belief that she is inadequate, arising from her childhood feelings of being overshadowed by her sister, will rear its ugly head. However, she has learned to challenge this belief, and not to listen when the voice of her inner child reacts and says, *I am inadequate.*

If we struggle with negative hidden beliefs, we also must challenge them and ask: *Whose voice am I listening to? Is it the real me, or just buried attitudes from the past, or a parent's voice? Who says I am unlovable?* Look at the facts and decide whether the belief you hold about yourself is true or not. If you think it is not, then you can work towards rejecting or changing it. This may take some time but is something that is possible.

Activity
Can you identify a hidden belief about yourself that causes you to become anxious?

Anxiety and goals

So why does anxiety arise in relation to goals? The answer lies in our ability to achieve that goal, rather than in the pursuit of the goal in itself. We are fine if the goal is within our reach, even if it means we have to push ourselves a bit to achieve it. If, however, the goal is not within our reach or appears uncertain, we can get very anxious, especially if our hidden belief is dependent upon that goal.

If the foundation for my self-worth rests on the belief that I must always be accepted and valued, or that I must always be clever, then when I fail to achieve these inflexible goals my anxiety levels are likely to soar. Also, such goals create problems because God made us to have our spiritual needs met in Him, and not only in being validated or affirmed by others. We need others to support us and encourage us, but we need our deeper spiritual needs met in God as well.

We can have goals for the various parts of our lives and these can be very helpful in making sure that we stay on track and achieve what we would like to. It is when the goal takes the place of God that issues arise. In Philippians 3:13-14 Paul talks about 'press[ing] on toward the goal to win the prize for which God [had] called [him]'. So maybe our main spiritual goal is to press on with God, but that does not mean that we can't have other goals related to our spirituality. It may also be that at times of high anxiety that goal is too hard to achieve – and that's OK.

Security in God

In order to cope with the uncertainties in life without our anxiety hitting the ceiling, it's important we focus our attention on learning how to meet our needs in God. When we are able to look to God and know that He is our Father and we are His children, we have an immense sense of security because He is always there for us.

> 'GOD, your God, is with you every step you take'
> **JOSH. 1:9, EUGENE PETERSON, *THE MESSAGE*.**

How reassuring to know that He is always with us, and that we are secure in His arms (Deut. 33:27) – whatever happens.

God showed how important we are to Him by sending His beloved Son Jesus to die for us. Think about how much you have understood this incredible truth. In God's eyes, we are worth sending Jesus to die for us! His death on the cross puts us in a totally secure place.

Again we can find our significance in God as Ephesians 2:10 reminds us that we are 'God's handiwork', and have been created 'to do good works'. When we focus on that and find our anchorage in God, it can help to lessen our anxiety and bring us peace.

Working towards more flexible goals

A major part of dealing with anxiety when it comes to goals, is to make our goals more flexible. If our goal is set in concrete and it looks like we will not achieve it, it is more likely to increase our anxiety. The use of words such as 'should', 'ought' and 'must' are unhelpful because they make demands of us or others in an unhealthy way.

For example, if your goal was to give a good presentation and you were constantly saying to yourself, *It must be OK, in fact it really should be perfect*, you would be demanding something of yourself that you may not be able to deliver. Your presentation may not be perfect and the PowerPoint or other technology may not work. As a result, your anxiety may rocket sky high because of having set such an inflexible goal.

However, if your goal was more flexible and you were able to say to yourself, *My goal is to do as good a job as I can, and my best is good enough*, even if it then all goes wrong, you can reassure yourself, that you did your best and that is all you can do. It can be helpful for you to remind yourself that perfection is not actually achievable and is often a very subjective concept anyway: what one person sees as perfect may not be so for someone else. If you can give yourself permission to have more flexible goals and to be good enough, then your anxiety levels are likely to be far lower. If you do have perfectionist tendencies, then you may need to practise this permission giving. With time you can become more relaxed and flexible in your goals.

We can also put high demands upon others by saying, '*They should do this*' or '*They ought to do that*' and if it's not done as we think it should be, we can become anxious. But who says they should or they ought? Our anxiety would be much lower if we were able to say to ourselves, *It would be preferable if they did this, but if they don't, it's not the end of the world. God can still work in this situation.*

In summary, to effectively counter the anxiety produced when our goal is not met, we need a flexible goal or, best of all, to have as

our goal the aim of meeting our deepest needs in God. To find out whether our goals will succeed in quenching our deep spiritual thirst for security and self-worth it's helpful to ask the following questions:
1. How rigid is that goal?
2. Will I reach that goal?
3. How important is that goal?
4. Where is God in that goal?

For Chris, her original goal of needing acceptance made her into a 'Yes' girl, the good girl in the class. She was afraid to disagree and her anxiety about whether people liked her or would reject what she had to offer made her an insecure person. Her inner belief was: *I am inadequate.*

However, now that Chris's goal is set on finding her security in God, her belief is based on statements such as: *I am of equal value and worth in God.* Whenever Chris finds herself getting anxious, she affirms her new belief and thinks, *Well, what's my goal? Why is it uncertain? Who else does it depend on? Where is God? How can I actually look to God in this and find my security in Him?* She has learned to be assertive and has found her voice.

Activity
Think of an event or person you feel anxious about and answer the following questions:

1. What is my goal?

_____

_____

2. What is happening that suggests the goal will not be reached or is uncertain? Why does it become uncertain (thereby increasing my anxiety)?

_____
_____

3. What is my belief about myself?

_____
_____

See if you can fit it together as a picture. Try to make sense of what you have discovered about yourself and how this relates to your anxiety. Can your goal become more flexible? Where is God? Perhaps He feels far away – how can you bring Him into the situation?

Reflection

While you may have been telling yourself that you are worthless, or some other negative message, this is not what the Bible says about those who love God. There are many verses that tell us how God sees us. Here are a few to begin with:

- I am a child of God. (John 1:12)
- I am Christ's friend. (John 15:15)
- I am a child of God, I can call Him my Father (or even Daddy!). (Romans 8:14–15)
- I am a temple for God's Holy Spirit living in me. (1 Cor. 3:16)
- I am a new person with my old life left behind. (2 Cor. 5:17)
- I am hidden with Christ in God. (Col. 3:3)

This is who you are in Christ. Read the list out loud and then choose one or two verses to memorise and use them next time you feel anxious. Think about Christ's death on the cross. What does that say about the way He feels about you? How does that sit with your feelings of worthlessness?

Prayer

Father, please help me not to look in all the wrong places to get my sense of self-worth and significance. Help me to look to You instead and find my identity in You. When I think that Jesus died on the cross for me, it makes me realise how much You love me and that in Your eyes I am very precious. Help me to remember next time I am tempted to be overcome by a sense of worthlessness that I am Your child and a member of Your family. You love me and You say that I am a Somebody, not a Nobody. That makes me feel so cherished. Thank You, Lord. Amen.

Chapter 3
How Anxiety Affects Us

> Some people feel guilty about their anxieties and regard them as a defect of faith. I don't agree at all. They are afflictions, not sins. Like all afflictions, they are, if we can so take them, our share in the Passion of Christ.
> **C.S. LEWIS**, *LETTERS TO MALCOLM: CHIEFLY ON PRAYER*[1]

Anxiety affects us in a number of different ways: in our bodies through the 'fight or flight' response with distressing symptoms such as sweating or feeling sick; in our thinking where we may experience unhelpful thoughts; and in our behaviour as we try to avoid or escape the anxiety. Looking at how anxiety affects us not only helps us understand what is going on during anxious times, but also gives us essential information on how to manage it.

Anxiety and our spiritual life
Our spiritual lives are affected when we become anxious. On the one hand, we are professing faith in God and yet, on the other hand it can seem that we are finding it difficult to grasp the truth of His

promises. Sometimes this apparent dilemma can have a knock-on effect on your relationship with God. It can be difficult to trust God when we are anxious and, added to that, we can end up feeling guilty about our anxiety. This can sometimes lead us to forget that God blesses us regardless of our weaknesses. If we can look at our anxieties from a different perspective, as C.S. Lewis says in the quotation at the start of this chapter, then we no longer have to feel guilty as we begin to see our anxieties are not a result of any defect in our faith.

People who are anxious and worried can find it hard to trust God, and, because their mind is not at peace, it can be difficult for them to pray and spend time in deepening their relationship with God. The words they say to themselves may sound like this: *I lack the faith to believe* and *I worry instead of believing*. This perspective reveals the belief that God won't respond to them or answer their prayers because they do not have enough faith. The misconception here is that God is dependent upon our faith to act. Since God is sovereign and self-determining, He invites us to have faith to believe but does not require this faith to act on our behalf. If we add to this the idea that anxieties are afflictions rather than lack of faith then, hopefully, this can allow for removal of feelings of guilt and a move towards peace with God.

It may also help anxiety sufferers to focus on what God has actually said about them and His activity on their behalf:

> O afflicted one, storm-tossed, and not comforted, I am about to set your stones in antimony, and lay your foundations with sapphires.
> ISAIAH 54:11, NRSV

> He delivers the afflicted by their affliction, and opens their ear by adversity. He also allured you out of distress into a

broad place where there was no constraint, and what was set on your table was full of fatness.
JOB 36:15–16, NRSV

He reached down from on high, he took me; he drew me out of mighty waters… He brought me out into a broad place; he delivered me because he delighted in me.
PSALM 18:16,19, NRSV

Even when a person's anxiety makes it hard for them to believe in God's action on their behalf and to see themselves as 'loved by Him', reading Bible verses such as these may be of help.

Anxiety and our bodies

PHYSIOLOGICAL CHANGES

One reason why anxiety is so feared by people is that it can have immense physical power. We hear people say things like, *I felt sick with worry* or *I was so nervous my hands were shaking*. This is because an emotional arousal of anxiety is triggered by an unconscious biochemical reaction from our autonomic nervous system (ANS).

The ANS regulates both the sympathetic and parasympathetic nervous systems, which work in contrasting ways. The sympathetic nervous system releases adrenalin and other hormones which gear us up for 'fight or flight' and charge our body up, while the parasympathetic nervous system slows our body down to rest.

It is the sympathetic nervous system that is automatically triggered if a person unexpectedly encounters a lion in the garden. Immediately, the brain perceives a dangerous threat to life, causing adrenalin to be released into the body and resulting in a burst of extra energy so that the threatened person can run much faster than normal to escape the danger.

Depending on the perceived level of threat and the likelihood of being able to fight or flee, our bodies may also 'freeze', which is almost like the body shutting down completely. Imagine a mouse that has been caught by a cat and 'plays dead'; unless the cat has not been fed it will tire of the very still mouse and leave it alone. The mouse is then able to run away. Fight, flight and freeze are all survival responses over which we have very little or no control.

Having said that, there are ways of training the body if you are someone who has a naturally anxious disposition. Breathing and relaxation techniques can be used to activate the parasympathetic nervous system and help to reduce anxiety levels. When you recognise that you are starting to get anxious, using these techniques can really help. They will be looked at in more detail in Chapter Five.

THE 'FIGHT OR FLIGHT' RESPONSE

Eyes and ears sense a threat

↓

This information is passed to the brain

↓

The brain goes on red alert and tells the adrenal glands (on the top of the kidneys) to release extra adrenalin into our blood vessels

↓

Blood vessels carry the adrenalin around the body

BODILY SYMPTOMS OF ANXIETY

The adrenalin carried around the body is responsible for wide-ranging physiological changes that can cause great embarrassment and fear in the anxiety sufferer as it appears that the body is totally out of control. These include:

- headaches and dizziness
- the pupils dilating, leading to blurred vision
- the mouth going dry, leading to difficulty swallowing
- the neck and shoulder muscles tensing, leading to aching neck and backache
- breathing becoming faster and shallower, supplying more oxygen to muscles (over-breathing, chest pain, tingling, palpitations, asthma)
- the heart beating more rapidly as it pumps harder to send oxygen and energy to muscles in preparation for flight
- blood pressure going up
- the sympathetic nervous system diverting blood from the skin, stomach and intestines (hence pale skin) to the heart, central nervous system and muscles because the body is preparing for action
- the stomach and guts shutting down, and the stomach feeling knotted or having 'butterflies' which may result in indigestion, loss of appetite, nausea and stomach upsets
- the liver releasing stored sugar to provide fuel for quick energy (excess energy in blood)
- the skin sweating to cool hot working muscles, leading to sweating, and blushing
- the muscles in use tensing and getting ready to react faster leading to tension, aches and pains in muscles, and 'the shakes'
- the sphincter relaxes, leading to frequent urination, diarrhoea.

> To many people cats are charming animals, but Sarah cannot stand them ever since she was badly clawed as a child by a neighbour's vicious tom. If she sees one, she is immediately overcome by a strong feeling of panic and will run as fast as she can in the opposite direction. The problem is that cats are actually quite common, and many family outings have been spoiled by Sarah's fear as, after a sighting, she is a physical wreck, shaking and exhausted, and needs to go to bed for several hours to get over the shock.

THE 'FIGHT OR FLIGHT' RESPONSE TO A THREAT

It can be enormously reassuring for anxiety sufferers to realise that their frightening symptoms are actually a normal response to a threat caused by the release of adrenalin into the body. It can also be helpful for them to realise that, as human beings, we do not have a lot of control over the autonomic nervous system. This means that they are not choosing to be anxious, but their anxiety is an automatic response to a perceived threat. Once they understand what is going on, they can normalise this process, and this in itself can lessen their anxiety.

The purpose of the physical reactions caused by the adrenalin is to increase our readiness for action by stimulating the 'fight or flight' hormone – the ideal state for someone who needs to react with a burst of energy.

For example, if you see a potentially violent person approach a little child in a car park, what do you do? Without even thinking about it, adrenalin is released, you snatch the child away from danger and run to safety with the child in your arms. However, once you have removed yourself from the impending threat, the burst of energy deserts you, and you become a nervous wreck. Your knees are knocking, your heart is pounding, and you feel like a quivering jelly because the adrenalin was only released in response to the very objective threat of someone's life in danger.

This normal response becomes a problem when the adrenalin is not only released in response to objective threats, but becomes stimulated by subjective threats which aren't really there but are actually more in our imagination or perceived threats about what might happen in the future.

> Ria had been sexually assaulted by a man in the street which left her feeling very afraid to go out. If she did go out, she had frequent panic attacks when she saw other men, convinced that they would sexually assault her too. All the evidence points to the fact that stranger assault is pretty rare, but Ria perceived the threat as high and her autonomic nervous system responded accordingly. There was not an actual threat to her, but she imagined that there was. Her body was simply protecting her from what she thought might happen, but it left her feeling anxious and unable to go out.

What can then happen is that the adrenalin button can be switched on and off so much that it becomes hypersensitive and can give us panic attacks any time, anywhere. This oversensitivity can also happen when we experience too many situations that cause us stress and anxiety.

Activity
When you are anxious, what physical symptoms do you experience?

_____

_____

Anxiety and unhelpful thoughts

PSYCHOLOGICAL CHANGES

However it starts, once anxiety is present, it is often maintained by how we perceive situations and what we say about them to ourselves. This next story shows differing responses to the same situation. Imagine two people who have worked for a long time for the same company. The company decides to undertake a restructure and both employees are made redundant and leave the organisation with a good sum of money. One of these people is distraught at being made redundant, thinks that their life is over, that they will never work again and, despite the money, that they will end up with financial problems. This person becomes extremely anxious about the future. The other person is disappointed at being made redundant and wonders what they might do now. They think that the money might help them to start a new business or at least tide them over until they can get another job. Their view of the future is that it can be an adventure and they feel excitement even if tinged with a tiny amount of anxiety. The different perceptions of the situation are the key to feeling OK about it as opposed to feeling terrible.

PSYCHOLOGICALLY-BIASED THINKING

Sometimes our thoughts are a distorted response to the information we receive, so that our opinions and perceptions are affected by a misinterpreted evaluation. The way we see the situation (which is not how it actually is) can then cause anxiety.

One of the challenges with anxious thoughts is that there can sometimes seem to be a grain of truth in them. For example, an anxious thought about failing can be kept alive by the reality that we rarely do things perfectly. Or a friend not having time for us this week can feed an anxious thought about being rejected. It is not that the anxious thought is really true, but that without realising it we are more alert to snippets of information that seem to confirm it is true in biased ways. If you've ever bought a new brand of car, you may have had the experience that suddenly you are seeing that brand on the road more than ever! Our thinking can be biased, particularly when it comes to looking for the negatives.

When we have these unhelpful types of thought, the anxiety is likely to be maintained. There are various types of unhelpful thinking styles or habits that can contribute to maintaining anxiety:

Prediction – Believing we know what's going to happen in the future or imagining that something bad will happen. With this way of thinking, we always predict that the worst will happen. Questions we might want to ask ourselves are: *Am I thinking that I can predict the future?' 'How likely is it that that might really happen?*

Mental filter – When we notice only what the filter allows or wants us to notice, and we dismiss anything that doesn't 'fit'. For example, if someone gives us positive feedback that might not fit with our view of ourselves, we dismiss it. Questions we might want to ask are: *Am I only noticing the bad stuff? Am I filtering out the positives? What would be more realistic?*

Judgments – Making evaluations or judgments about events, ourselves, others, or the world, rather than describing what we actually see and have evidence for. Alternative thoughts might be: *I'm making an evaluation about the situation or person. It's how I make sense of the world, but that doesn't mean my judgments are always right or helpful. Is there another perspective?*

Emotional reasoning – *I feel bad so it must be bad! I feel anxious, so I must be in danger.* Alternative thoughts might be: *Just because it feels bad, doesn't necessary mean it is bad. My feelings are just a reaction to my* *thoughts – and thoughts are just automatic brain reflexes.*

Mind-reading – Assuming we know what others are thinking (usually about us). Generally we think that others are being critical of us, and this can feed into our anxiety. For example: *They are thinking that I am doing a really bad job.* A thought such as this is likely to feed our anxiety. It might be helpful, as an alternative, to ask what the evidence is that others are thinking negatively about us. Also, it would be helpful to recognise that these are our thoughts, not theirs, and to consider what a more balanced view might be.

Mountains and molehills – Some anxiety comes from an inaccurate evaluation of the size of the task to be completed and our ability to do so. Exaggerating the risk of danger, or exaggerating the negatives and minimising the positives and our ability to cope, can lead to anxiety. So do ask: *Am I exaggerating the bad stuff? How would someone else see it? What would be their view of my ability?*

Catastrophising – Imagining, believing and convincing ourselves that the worst possible thing will happen. If we believe that the worst will happen, this is very likely to increase feelings of anxiety. As an alternative, it may be helpful to think about the likelihood of what we most fear actually happening.

Shoulds and musts – Thinking or saying *I should (or shouldn't)* and *I must* puts pressure on ourselves, and sets up unrealistic expectations. This pressure can lead us to feel more anxious. This links with the goal setting that we saw in the last chapter. We need to be flexible and have realistic expectations of ourselves.

All or nothing thinking – Believing that something or someone can be only good or bad, right or wrong, rather than anything in between. This can lead to us putting pressure on ourselves that we are good or bad, right or wrong, and this can feed our anxiety. It is helpful to realise that things aren't either totally white or totally black; there are shades of grey and that's OK.

To help anybody with these sorts of anxiety problems, we must identify what their thinking pattern is, and show them that, far from freeing themselves from anxiety, they are actually making the problem worse by maintaining and feeding the unhelpful thought patterns.

> Tricia was the first one in her family to go to university. She felt anxious about fitting in as she was from a working-class background and thought the other students would be from 'posh schools'. She was also worried about whether she would be able to do the work needed to obtain a degree. Tricia's anxiety took her to the student counselling service where she worked with a counsellor to change her unhelpful thinking and so reduce her anxiety. Tricia went on to graduate with a good degree and had a good group of friends while she was a student.

Activity
Write down the sort of thoughts you have when you feel anxious:
_____
_____

Anxiety and our behaviour

BEHAVIOURAL MAINTAINING CYCLES
The Anxiety Curve diagram on the next page helps us to see what actually happens in our behaviour in relation to anxiety. If you were

to ask a group of people: *What would happen if you were to remain in the situation you fear? Would your anxiety stay the same, increase or decrease?* most anxious people would answer *increase*. They fear that, if their anxiety continues rising, something terrible will happen, perhaps that they will faint, vomit, have a heart attack, or go mad. On the graph they imagine the line rising sharply until it goes off the page and they 'explode'.

However, this belief is not right. Experience and experiments with anxious people show that after a certain time the anxiety begins to decrease of its own accord. Therefore, the more an anxious person faces the fear, the more the initial anxiety decreases and so does the time the anxiety lasts for. The graph below shows how an anxious person's anxiety will diminish as they expose themselves to small targets. Putting oneself into anxiety-provoking situations using anxiety management skills is an important way forward in overcoming some types of anxiety.

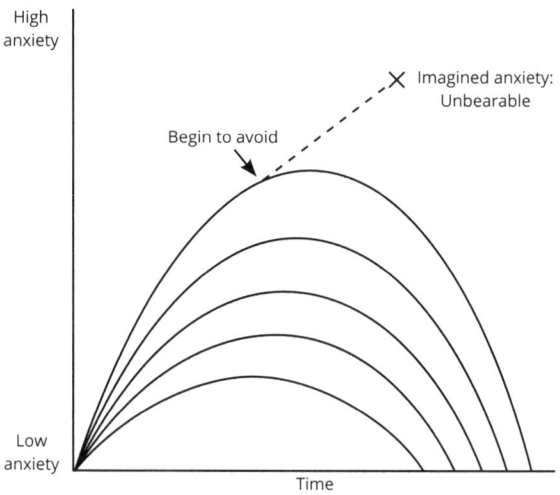

Anxiety curve and avoidance diagram

1. Avoidance and escape

One of the natural reactions to perceived danger is to flee from it, or avoid it. This is the 'fight or flight' response. However, avoidance of, and escape from perceived dangers simply maintain anxiety because they prevent a person from learning how to manage the anxiety. If you never do the thing that you are anxious about, you never learn that your worst predictions do not come true. You also do not learn that anxiety is not as harmful to you physically as you might think. As you confront what makes you anxious, generally you will, with time, become less anxious.

2. Seeking reassurance (positive reinforcer)

'Reassurance seeking' can also subtly fuel anxiety. The person who constantly seeks reassurance to boost their confidence will frequently ask, *Am I doing OK?* However, this actually indicates that the person subconsciously doubts that they or the situation will be OK and, because of this, it will not be long before they feel the need to seek reassurance again.

Although wanting to be reassured is a very natural tendency, it does not actually help anxiety. Chris once worked with a dentist who wanted to help some patients get over needle phobia. Before seeking her help, the dentist had been giving them tranquillisers, not realising that this was actually a positive reinforcement, because the people with needle phobia never had to face their anxiety. Again, the patients could only find release from their heightened anxiety levels by facing their needle phobia and working through it.

While recognising that reassurance alone will never solve the root problem and that anxiety sufferers must face their fears to move on, it is not a good idea to totally abandon the anxiety sufferer in their anxious situation with the attitude that they need tosink or swim – a process called 'flooding'. Chris prefers a gentler approach where people are gradually exposed to their anxiety, getting them to move on step by step rather than expecting them to progress in one gigantic leap.

3. Social maintaining cycles

Anxiety can also be maintained through social support. One example of the social maintaining cycle which nurtures a subtle (and well-meaning) maintenance of the anxiety problem is the kindly friend who does an agoraphobic person's shopping, thus allowing the sufferer to remain at home and avoid facing their fear. Such 'helpful' behaviour, although motivated by generosity, actually contributes to maintaining the anxiety in the longer term, and fails to help the sufferer move on. What would be more helpful is for the agoraphobic person to be encouraged little by little to go outside, maybe with the friend's support. On each occasion that they go out, they could go a little further until the agoraphobic person is able to go shopping. This 'little and often' approach to dealing with the anxiety-provoking event is known as 'graded exposure'. Generally people will need support if they are going to try this approach.

> Yetunde was a great believer in 'loving your neighbour' and was known for her good deeds in her church and neighbourhood. When she heard that Ros had agoraphobia, Yetunde quickly became indispensable, dropping everything to be with Ros if she needed to go out anywhere. Yetunde was very upset when she was told that her actions were more harmful than helpful, but she followed the advice she was given, and when Ros rang, she told her firmly that she could not accompany her.
>
> 'It really upset me,' said Yetunde. 'Ros thought I didn't want to be her friend anymore, and sometimes she would be crying and pleading for me to help her. It was so hard to turn that plea for help down.' However, as Ros gradually

> overcame her phobia, she realised that Yetunde had actually behaved like a true friend, and one of her first trips on her own was to have coffee at Yetunde's house.

Activity
Can you identify your avoidance and escape behaviour when anxious?

_____
_____

Reflection
Read Mark 4:35–41. Imagine the scene. Picture the storm, the howling gale and the fishing boat tossing on the huge waves, with water crashing over the deck and soaking the disciples. They are terrified at the force of the storm and fear for their lives.
- Where is Jesus in their fear?
- Does He abandon them to their fear?
- What happens to the storm when the disciples cry out to Him for help?
- Why were they so afraid even though Jesus was with them?

Now picture the anxiety that is causing you distress as though it is the storm and visualise yourself in the boat that is in the midst of the turmoil.
- How intense is the anxiety storm? How high are its waves? What is happening to your boat?
- Where is Jesus?
- What does He say to the anxiety storm?
- What is the atmosphere in the boat if Jesus is there? What happens to the waves and wind?

- Why are you so afraid? Can you sense His peace?

Prayer

Dear God, thank You that even when my mind and body make me feel as though I am in the midst of a raging storm and I am terrified that the waves of anxiety will overwhelm me, I am not on my own. Even though sometimes the sounds of the raging waves and howling wind distract me from the sense of Your presence, I know that You are there with me. I pray that just as You calmed the winds and waves when the disciples were shaking with fear, You will bring me also into calm waters. Strengthen my faith, I pray, and help me to believe that when You said, 'Quiet! Be still!' I can experience that deep peace within my own life. Amen.

Chapter 4

Understanding Specific Anxieties

> Worry doesn't empty tomorrow of its sorrow. It empties today of its strength.
> **CORRIE TEN BOOM, *CLIPPINGS FROM MY NOTEBOOK*[1]**

Worry appears to be insubstantial when we try to pin it down, but it can have devastating effects upon the sufferer and those close to them, preventing people from living their lives to the full, and making them slaves to their anxiety. In this chapter we will be looking at specific anxieties in more detail, such as panic attacks, social anxiety, health anxiety and generalised anxiety disorder (GAD), and the effect they have on our lives.

Awareness of anxiety levels

Becoming aware of the level of their anxiety helps educate people in the importance of keeping their anxiety below a certain level to prevent panic attacks.

There are various self-help websites that can help you to become more aware of the anxiety you experience. These can help you to spot the signs so that you can help yourself before the anxiety becomes too strong (for example: getselfhelp.co.uk).

A continuum for panic attack symptoms

Relaxation
Feeling at ease and at peace

Marked anxiety
Feeling about to lose control, heart beating faster, muscles tight

Major panic attack
Terror, fear of going crazy, or dying

The first signs of anxiety can be quite small, and may be experienced as fleeting twinges of concern, gradually increasing in strength. Butterflies in the stomach and palpitations may follow and, as the heart beats stronger and faster and palms begin to sweat, there is often a real fear of being out of control. At this stage, the rising anxiety can be called 'marked anxiety' because it is here that anxiety becomes more of a problem. The frightened sufferer senses that they are losing control. They fear fainting (a perceived loss of control) and because they seem to have no power over what their body is doing, they are terrified of having a panic attack, which may then actually occur. However, by understanding where their symptoms are on a continuum, people can more easily identify the level of anxiety they have reached. By understanding what is happening to them, they are then far more likely to be able to use strategies to stop panic attacks before the anxiety reaches that level.

Panic attacks

To ascertain whether a person is actually suffering a panic attack, it can be useful to use the continuum above and think *Where is this person on the continuum?*

However, one of the most useful assessments is the diagnostic health tool[2] below. The true panic attack is characterised by a period of intense anxiety, fear or discomfort in which four (or more) of the symptoms described below develop abruptly and reach a peak within ten minutes:

- Chest pain or discomfort
- Sensations of shortness of breath or smothering
- Palpitations, pounding heart, or accelerated heart rate
- Sweating
- Chills or hot flushes
- Feelings of choking
- Nausea or abdominal distress
- Trembling or shaking
- Numbness or a tingling sensation
- Feeling dizzy, unsteady, light-headed, or faint
- Feelings of unreality or being detached from oneself
- Fear of losing control or going crazy
- Fear of dying

The panic attack experience

Never underestimate how terrifying it is to experience a panic attack, an experience not helped by well-meaning friends saying things like *Oh, don't be so silly* or *Get a grip*. Although panic attacks generally last only a few minutes, their severity makes them seem to last an eternity to the sufferer, especially as some unfortunate people may have a succession of panic attacks one after the other.

Panic attacks can also make people feel very ashamed, so it's important to normalise the whole experience, and help them understand what's actually going on in their body. It can be tremendously releasing to discover that the panic attack is simply a normal physiological reaction to anxiety that has got out of control.

A common pattern is that sufferers may have been going through a very stressful time in their lives, but when 18 months later they suddenly start having panic attacks, they fail to connect the two things. What seems to happen is that the body is overstressed by coping with too much, so the adrenalin button becomes overly sensitive. Normalising what is happening is a major step in helping people to start switching off this 'fight or flight' switch.
The beliefs and fears that fuel most panic attacks include:

- I am going to die from a heart attack.
- I am going to die from suffocation.
- I am going to have a stroke.
- I am going to faint and make a fool of myself.
- I am going crazy and having a nervous breakdown.
- I am losing control.
- I feel so weak I cannot move, and I am frightened of falling.
- I am embarrassed by this, I feel ashamed of myself.

These feelings are very real to people, especially the fear of dying, but such beliefs and fears simply feed the anxiety and make it even worse. In addition to this, panic attacks can seem to come 'out of the blue' and so can seem totally out of the person's control and this can make them even more frightening. Thus, it is often beneficial to help the anxious person identify the beliefs and fears underlying their panic attacks, and challenge the distortions contained in them.

The cycle of panic

In panic attacks there can be a cycle of panic within the person's life. Firstly, the person experiences some sort of trigger. For example, they feel worried about the previous day's work and fear the boss's anger, making them anxious about going to work.

They then get a physical reaction at work such as chest pains, breathlessness or dizziness.

The next stage is increasing distress because of the physical symptoms they are experiencing with accompanying panicky thoughts: *I must be going mad* or *I'm going to have a heart attack* or *I will collapse. I can't cope.* However, when they start thinking like this, it only increases the stress and their anxiety. Finally, the panic button goes off and they go into a full-blown panic attack, making them say to themselves, *I fear the fear because my body is getting out of control.*

This increases the physical reaction even more, and the whole process often repeats in a vicious circle of fear that becomes very hard for the sufferer to break, even though they find it so incapacitating. In this way, going to work (or whatever the anxiety provoking event is) becomes a 'trigger' for panic which could mean that even thinking about work causes real anxiety and potentially an actual panic attack.

> Malcolm will never forget the first time he had a panic attack. He was a high-powered businessman and had been working long hours on a stressful project that would result in further promotion if successful. However, Malcolm was so anxious about achieving the deadline that he was having difficulty sleeping, wasn't eating properly, and was surviving by drinking copious amounts of black coffee. As the deadline got nearer, his stress levels got higher and higher, and suddenly he had such severe pains in his chest that he could hardly breathe. 'My vision was blurred, I was sweating heavily, and I couldn't hear because my ears were ringing. I thought I was dying.' The doctor reassured Malcolm that it was stress and not a heart attack, but a few days later he had another attack, and since then they have happened on a fairly regular basis.

An insight into Anxiety

> Paralysed by fear at the thought of experiencing further panic attacks at work, Malcolm has had to leave his high-flying job and feels depressed and isolated.

The cycle of panic is illustrated in the diagram below.

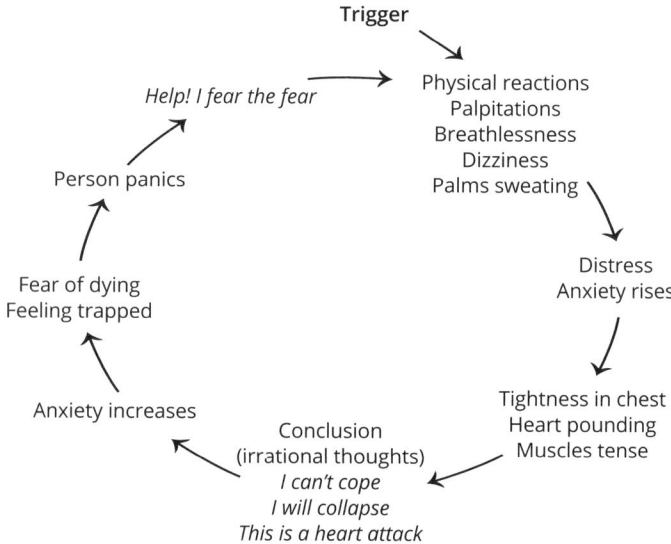

Ways to manage panic attacks

The best way to treat panic attacks, which may or may not involve hyperventilating (see below), is to understand what is happening and then face the fear with graded exposure. Forewarned is definitely forearmed in the case of the panic attack.

Steps to managing a panic attack
1. Give understanding of the physiology.
2. Identify the triggers (if any).
3. Teach a breathing exercise (p76).
4. Teach a relaxation exercise (Appendix 2).

5. Identify destructive thoughts and beliefs (p80).
6. Teach the use of thought records (p82).
7. Teach distraction techniques (p87).
8. Plan step-by-step exposure to the trigger (collaboratively).

Hyperventilation

About 70% of panic attacks are accompanied by acute hyperventilation, although it can also be a common reaction when we experience other strong emotions such as fear, excitement and anger.

Hyperventilation simply means over-breathing, ie breathing in excess of your body's needs. This is a relatively common problem, so it is useful to know how to help people when they hyperventilate.

PHYSIOLOGY OF NORMAL BREATHING

Firstly, we need to know what happens during the process of normal breathing.
1. When you breathe you take in oxygen.
2. Haemoglobin in the blood carries the oxygen to the tissues.
3. Body cells use the oxygen.
4. Carbon dioxide is released as a by-product.
5. Carbon dioxide is then carried back to the lungs where it is breathed out.

PHYSIOLOGY OF HYPERVENTILATION

When adrenalin surges through your body in response to a perceived threat, the muscles are tightened and it becomes more difficult to breathe properly. At this point over-breathing will occur because the body's natural response to danger is to supply the muscles with more oxygen in order that the 'fight or flight' mechanism can take effect. When you begin to over-breathe, the balance of gases in the lungs is upset. A small amount of carbon dioxide normally stays in the lungs. If you breathe in too much air too often, the carbon dioxide is pushed out. This is what can cause some of the symptoms associated with hyperventilation.

Let's look at the process in more detail.

There is rapid, shallow breathing from the chest rather than from the diaphragm.

Symptoms occur because there is too little carbon dioxide in the lungs, and the blood becomes more alkaline.

Eventually, if rapid breathing continues, the body may cut off this excessive supply of oxygen by causing us to faint.

It causes large amounts of oxygen to be taken into the lungs which means that the heart must beat even faster to cope.

Changes in the balance between oxygen and carbon dioxide occur in the lungs.

Rapid breathing in pushes out the carbon dioxide which normally forms a reservoir in the lungs.

This in turn leads to vascular constriction, resulting in diminished blood flow to the brain and other parts of the body.

When we faint we return to normal patterns of breathing, so fainting is a 'fail-safe' way of controlling hyperventilation.

During this time, a person's attention tends to be focused only on the fact that they are finding it hard to breathe and not on anything else. This narrowing of their focus can be unhelpful as it reinforces all the worry they are experiencing. It would be more useful if they could move their attention to things around them. This can help them to think about more than just their breathing and help them to ground themselves in the reality that none of the awful things they are thinking are true.

SYMPTOMS OF HYPERVENTILATION

The symptoms caused by hyperventilation can be distressing. Because we are breathing so rapidly it makes it hard to catch our breath, and so we may attempt to compensate by over-breathing because we think that will alleviate the tightness in the chest.

Symptoms such as light-headedness, feeling faint, the feeling of unreality, tingling in the limbs, and rigid or spasming muscles, are caused by the lack of carbon dioxide in the lungs.

Other symptoms include:
- sudden emotional outbursts
- feeling too hot or too cold

- weakness
- numbness
- fatigue
- chest pain
- sweating
- clammy hands
- tremors
- swallowing difficulties.

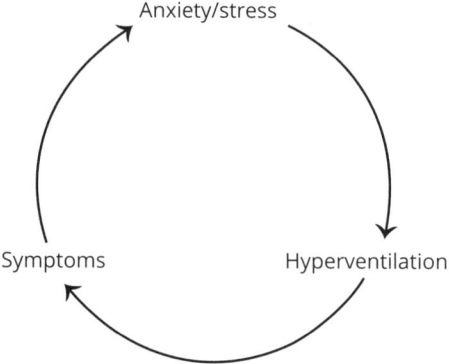

WAYS TO STOP HYPERVENTILATION

Fortunately, although hyperventilation produces frightening symptoms, there are specific techniques that can bring welcome relief to the sufferer. Two things must happen in order to stop hyperventilation. Firstly, we need to help the sufferer stop over-breathing, and secondly, we need to get enough carbon dioxide back into their lungs to restore the correct balance.

When someone is hyperventilating, first get them to stop whatever they are doing. Keep calm (fear is infectious), and speak slowly, firmly and quietly. Ask them to hold their breath for as long as they comfortably can, about ten to fifteen seconds, as this will prevent the dissipation of carbon dioxide. If they can manage to do this, repeat several times, but be aware that their state of anxiety may already be too high.

One of the best ways to help hyperventilation is to teach the anxious person to cup their hands together and make a seal over their nose and mouth. Then encourage the person to breathe in through their nose (if possible) and breathe out hard through their mouth. This allows the carbon dioxide that they exhale to be breathed back into their system, correcting the balance. The person should continue to breathe in and out slowly and naturally, repeating the process four to five times (no more), by which time they should be feeling a bit better.

Some people have hyperventilation syndrome, which is breathing in excess of the body's requirements. This is a chronic condition, rather than the acute condition which we have been focusing on so far. The reduced amount of carbon dioxide in the blood from ongoing over-breathing can lead to physiological problems and needs to be treated by a professional.

From an acute occurrence of hyperventilation, as the person begins to feel more in control, encourage them as they breathe to make the out-breaths longer than the in-breaths. This helps to activate the relaxation response (parasympathetic nervous system) and causes the arousal response (sympathetic nervous system) to lessen. The reason this happens is because there are neurons in the brain that will send signals to the brain's arousal system. Scientists at Stanford University[3] discovered that if we slow breathing down, then the neurons do not signal the arousal centre and so calming breathing can also calm the mind.

If someone is hyperventilating, begin at a rate that feels comfortable to them, perhaps starting at breathing in for the count of three and out for six, then increasing to five/eight. For those who suffer from panic attacks, it is also a good idea to practise this breathing technique for around ten minutes twice daily.

Another helpful way to stop hyperventilation is vigorous exercise – while breathing in and out through the nose, run, briskly walk, or run up and down stairs. A simple adjustment of the person's posture (if sitting or standing) so that elbows are on a level with or above the shoulders will also make it difficult to over-breathe. Later on in this book, in Chapter 5, you will find a specific breathing exercise. By practising this regularly, you can ensure that the body will have what it needs in terms of oxygen and carbon dioxide, and hopefully hyperventilation will not occur.

Don't get upset if the person having the attack gets emotional, a common by-product of the high anxiety responsible for the panic attack. Try not to get involved in an argument or disagreement, and don't tell them off, but keep reassuring them with phrases like 'It's OK, it's going to be all right' and 'Take your time and just breathe', while physical touch (eg stroking the upper shoulder) may also have a calming effect. However, there are people for whom physical touch can be very triggering, so permission for touch probably needs to be sought. After the attack has finished, treat the person in the same way as someone in shock, with rest and a sweet drink, and if you still feel worried, call their doctor.

Specific types of anxiety

GENERALISED ANXIETY DISORDER (GAD)

Generalised anxiety disorder (GAD) is the feeling of being anxious about almost everything and anything for no particular, apparent reason. Often, people affected by GAD will feel overly worried about a wide range of things relating to a variety of topics including health, money, work, school and relationships. GAD is therefore a condition which leaves people feeling anxious about a multitude of things rather than any one specific thing. While most of us worry or feel anxious at some point in our lives, those who experience generalised anxiety find it particularly difficult to control their worries. On the whole, their feelings of anxiety are more persistent and often begin to affect their daily lives.

The NICE website suggests that the prevalence of GAD in the UK is about 1 in 23 people. It is diagnosed through typical symptoms that exist for at least six months or that occur every day for several months.

There are both psychological and physical symptoms of GAD. Psychological symptoms include:

- restlessness
- a sense of dread
- feeling constantly on edge
- difficulty concentrating
- irritability.

Physical symptoms include:

- dizziness
- tiredness
- muscle aches and tension
- trembling or shaking
- excessive sweating
- palpitations
- problems sleeping
- shortness of breath
- stomach ache
- feeling sick
- headaches.

Symptoms can be mild or more acute and some of them may be felt much of the time. It is common for GAD sufferers to think they are going mad but, like all anxiety disorders, the condition is not connected to insanity. Relaxation exercises can help but, if

PHOBIAS

Phobias represent some of the most extreme forms of anxiety. They are also one of the most common forms of anxiety. According to the NHS, about 10,000,000 people in the UK have a phobia. This equates to 14.6% of the population or roughly 1 in 7 people. The dictionary definition of the word phobia is 'An abnormal or morbid fear or aversion.'[4] A phobia is a persistent and irrational fear of a specific thing or situation that compels the sufferer to avoid it at all costs, even when they are given the awareness and reassurance that it is not dangerous. You can become phobic about absolutely anything, and phobia sufferers will go to extreme lengths to avoid situations or objects that they fear.

Phobias are extremely distressing but unfortunately have become the butt of jokes online and in social media. This can mean that people who suffer from phobias do not always get taken seriously by others, but they are serious; some phobias can have a very detrimental effect on the individual. Once a phobia has become established in the mind of a person, the best way to overcome it is to persevere in slowly facing up to the crippling fear that the person experiences. A step-by-step planned exposure to the phobia is the usual form of treatment, and has an excellent success rate if the person is able to complete the process.

Agoraphobia

Agoraphobia is a fairly common and also potentially life-narrowing phobia. It is an abnormal fear of open spaces or public places. The agoraphobic fears being in any situation or place where they do not feel safe or where they feel trapped. This fear urges them to escape to a place of safety which is normally their own home. The fear usually reflects an expectation that something terrible will happen to them as an individual, to their loved ones, or to their property. Some sufferers find that they can venture further away from their place of safety if accompanied by a trusted friend or relative. However, the agoraphobic may then become so totally reliant upon their 'carer' that they can no longer go out without help.

The agoraphobic's fear may sometimes be so overwhelming that it triggers a panic attack. This experience with its awful physiological sensations in addition to the original fear may then make it almost impossible for the sufferer to leave the safety of their home. Although understandable, this course of action actually reinforces the fear and makes recovery much harder. It is important that the sufferer realises that their brain has become conditioned, and that what has been learned can also be unlearned. Generally, the only way forward is some form of exposure programme which will help them to face the fear.

> Joan, 45, has been happily married for 25 years and has two teenage children. Since she experienced a panic attack while shopping in town – an experience she described as 'being totally reduced to a quivering jelly of fear' – she has been unable to leave the house unless someone is with her. Even a trip to the corner shop five minutes away has become impossible, and she no longer visits friends for coffee, becoming more and more isolated within her own four walls. Although Joan feels very guilty about the stress her condition is causing her family, she is unable to visualise a day when she will ever be able to go out on her own again.

Other specific phobias

There are clear criteria that are helpful in deciding whether a person is suffering from a phobia. The phobia sufferer will characteristically show marked and persistent fear that is unreasonable or excessive, triggered by the anticipation or presence of a specific situation or object. If the sufferer is then exposed to the feared situation or object, it almost invariably provokes a strong and immediate anxiety response, and possibly a panic attack. In children, this anxiety may be expressed through crying, tantrums or clinging when faced with a feared situation or object. Phobia sufferers will do everything possible to avoid the phobic situation or, if there is no other option, exhibit intense anxiety and distress in the presence of their fear. Specific phobias include:

- animals
- natural features of the environment, such as heights, storms or water
- blood – injections
- situations such as flying, using lifts, or being in enclosed spaces (eg the cinema)
- situations that may lead to choking, vomiting or contact with an illness
- in children, loud sounds or costumed characters.

Social anxiety

Social anxiety is characterised by a person's fear of negative evaluation, which the person feels will result from some form of failed performance. This is performance in its broadest sense and includes emotional control skills and the performance of everyday tasks in which the person may be worried about the views of those around them. This could include eating in public, signing your name or speaking in a group. The worry is that you will say or do something that will cause others to judge you negatively. It is extremely inhibiting, and makes the person hypersensitive to their own behaviour as they continually worry what others are thinking about them. Actually, sufferers rarely behave in a way that will cause others to judge them negatively, but they will 'avoid' social contact just in case they do.

For teenagers under 18 years, it is important that symptoms last for at least six months before a diagnosis of social anxiety is made, as many teenagers are naturally self-conscious in public. Social anxiety may include behaviours such as:

- fear of public speaking
- fear of eating in public
- fear of urinating in public
- fear of blushing.

It is thought that up to 20% of introverts suffer with social anxiety Their natural temperament and personality often result in a slow attainment of social confidence, and therefore some sufferers find it beneficial to undergo training in social skills, working on their perception of social situations and what their role is. Having said that, it is entirely possible for extraverts to experience social anxiety too.

> Sienna, aged 23, has developed social anxiety and still lives at home with her parents. As a child she moved frequently because her father was in the army and this hindered her development of social skills, especially as she was often bullied at school because her accent was different and she was quite plump. As a result, Sienna began to stutter at school and her mind would go blank if the teacher asked her a question. Sienna began to get more and more anxious about seeming stupid.
>
> The problem has not improved as she's got older. Sienna is afraid to talk to people in case they find her boring or stupid, and if she goes out to a social occasion

> she will worry about it for hours beforehand, and then for hours afterwards analyse every minute detail of her behaviour. She feels so tense that nowadays she almost never goes out at all, and avoids people whenever she can. Consequently her workmates think that she is rude and stuck up.

Other types of anxiety

Health anxiety

The clinical name for this type of anxiety is hypochondriasis and it is actually classified as a somatoform disorder. This means that the person experiences physical symptoms that suggest physical illness or injury, but the symptoms are not actually attributable to a medical condition. The symptoms that result from a somatoform disorder are due to mental factors. In people who have a somatoform disorder, medical test results are either normal or do not explain the person's symptoms. Patients with this disorder often become worried about their health because the doctors are unable to find a cause for their health problems. Symptoms are sometimes similar to those of other illnesses and may last for several years. In many cases what is happening is that the person is misinterpreting bodily sensations and coming to the conclusion that they have something seriously wrong with them. For example, someone who has a blood pressure test is told they their blood pressure is in the normal range and should be checked again at a later date. The person may decide that the very idea of needing to be checked again means that there is something wrong with them. They thus remain anxious about their health.

Treatment is focused on helping the person manage their unhelpful thoughts and accepting the more benign explanations for their symptoms that they are likely to be offered. If the anxiety around health is extreme, the person may need professional help, which is likely to consist of talking therapy, possibly together with medication for the anxiety.

Post-traumatic stress disorder (PTSD)

PTSD used to be classified as an anxiety disorder, but has now been classified as a trauma and stress related disorder. However, people who suffer from PTSD may well also suffer from anxiety. As with most anxiety, this is often related to fear of what will happen. Army veterans have reported being retraumatised on 5th November by the bangs of fireworks which take them back to their tours of duty in war zones. People who have been sexually violated or physically assaulted may become anxious about having to leave the house alone for fear of the assault happening again. It can be quite common for people with PTSD to experience panic attacks due to the level of fear they experience. If the PTSD is particularly severe, the person may have very vivid flashbacks such that they feel as though they are in the traumatising situation again. If you, as a helper, are with someone who goes into flashback, being there for them and reassuring them in a quiet, calm voice can be helpful in bringing them back from the past into the present. If you as an individual feel yourself going into flashback you can try to ground yourself by touching things around you, by noticing the colour of your walls or furniture. If you have a pet, stroking them and noticing the feel of their fur or skin can help. By doing these things you are focusing on the here and now which can help to stop you from going back to the past. The information in the previous sections on panic attacks and hyperventilation will also be relevant to PTSD sufferers, and it can be helpful for the sufferer to receive professional help to overcome PTSD.

Separation anxiety

We commonly hear about separation anxiety with regard to young children when they have to leave their parents. Indeed, separation anxiety and fear of strangers is common in young children between the ages of six months and three years, but it's a normal part of a child's development and they usually grow out of it. However, it is also possible to experience separation anxiety as an adult and this is more likely if you also experienced it as a child. People with adult separation anxiety experience high levels of anxiety, and sometimes even panic attacks, when loved ones are out of reach.

People with this type of anxiety may be socially withdrawn, or show extreme sadness or difficulty concentrating when away from loved ones. In parents, this type of anxiety can lead to strict, over-involved parenting. In relationships, you may be more likely to be an overbearing partner. These last two examples are because you are likely to want to know where the loved person is at all times and to be sure they are safe. For your loved ones however this level of monitoring can become overwhelming and suffocating, and they may think you do not trust them.

Other common symptoms include:

- unfounded fears that loved ones, or yourself, will be abducted or fatally injured
- extreme and persistent hesitancy or refusal to leave the proximity of loved ones
- difficulty sleeping away from a loved one for fear that something will happen to them
- depression or anxiety attacks related to any of the above topics.

You may also have physical aches and pains, headaches, and diarrhoea associated with periods of anxiety. Unhelpful thinking is again a key factor with this type of anxiety, so working on changing thoughts to more realistic ones is helpful. You may also want to think about trying new ways of behaving such as not asking all the

'Where have you been?' and 'What were you doing?' questions when a loved one has been out for a while.

We have been putting labels on anxiety and talking about how anxieties are classified. This is to try to aid understanding. At the end of the day though, it is what you, or the person you are helping, are feeling that is the key thing. You don't have to put a label on everything, although some people find them helpful, but you may need to work on what is causing your anxiety and your associated thoughts and feelings, so that it will decrease.

Activity
Have you struggled with any of these specific anxieties? If so, from what you have learned so far, how can you help yourself?

_____

_____

_____

Reflection
Look at the following two passages:

Isaiah 43:1-2
- What does God say of Israel? (v1). Read the verse out loud and replace the names of Jacob and Israel with your own. Why does God tell us not to fear?
- What sort of situations does God tell us He will be with us in? Do you think these are situations that would cause anxiety? Picture God with you in your situation. Picture Him being with you – in the waters, through the rivers, in the fire, through the flames – carrying you.

Matthew 6:25–34
- Go for a walk or sit in your garden and look around you at the trees, flowers, animals and birds, or watch a natural history programme on the television. Read this passage slowly and take inspiration from the way that God cares for His natural creation. How much are you worth to your Father? How much was He willing to pay for you? What does this passage suggest as an antidote to worry (v33)?

Prayer

Thank You, God, that You call me by my name and I am Yours. Thank You that You will be with me when it seems that I am walking through a fiery furnace as I struggle to deal with my emotions, and that I do not need to be afraid because You are my Redeemer. Thank You also for the beauty of Your creation that brings me peace in my darkest moments. Thank You that I am fearfully and wonderfully made, and that if I submit myself to Your loving hands, You are able to reshape me and turn me into a beautiful vessel that reflects Your glory. Amen.

Chapter 5
Skills to Help Overcome Anxiety

> Sow a thought,
> Reap an action:
> Sow an action,
> Reap a habit:
> Sow a habit,
> Reap a character:
> Sow a character,
> Reap a destiny.
> **RALPH WALDO EMERSON**[1]

Skills and strategies are available to deal successfully with all sorts of anxiety disorders including generalised anxiety disorder, phobias and social anxiety. As the Waverley Integrative Framework illustrates, we are made up of different areas, and there are strategies to help us, physically, emotionally, behaviourally, mentally and spiritually. By persevering in the use of these skills, the stranglehold of your anxiety will, in all likelihood, begin to loosen, although sometimes people with acute anxiety may also require medication or professional support in the form of counselling to help them function well enough to work on using these anxiety management skills.

Anxiety and our bodies: changing our physical response

SKILLS TO REDUCE PHYSICAL SYMPTOMS OF ANXIETY

1. Breathing

As we saw earlier when we looked at hyperventilation, managing breathing is a key way to manage anxiety and its effects. Practising the breathing exercise below on a daily basis can really help to reduce anxious feelings such that you probably will not need to deal with hyperventilation as it is likely you won't reach that point.

Activity

BREATHING EXERCISE: BREATHING OURSELVES CALM
Make sure you are sitting comfortably with your feet slightly apart, and with your eyes closed or looking down. Be aware of the chair taking your weight, and become responsive to how still you are, ignoring noises or intrusive thoughts. Try putting any distractions away in an imaginary box; just think of peace and calm.

Now become aware of your slow breathing, in and out of your nose, and continue for a few breaths. Note whether you find the in-breath (inhalation) or out-breath (exhalation) more comfortable. Continue to breathe slowly. Now count how long your in-breath is and how long your out-breath is. Carry on breathing to identify this rhythm, and stay with it.

Continuing with your in-breath the same, make your out-breath about two counts longer (eg if your in-breath is a slow three, make your out-breath five). Stay with this, breathing gently without forcing any breaths. Every time you breathe out, do it slowly with a sigh, rather like a balloon deflating. Continue for a few more minutes to deeply breathe and relax. Note how much more relaxed the body is, and how your anxiety is reducing.

2. Relaxation

Relaxation is incompatible with feeling anxious because relaxation is controlled by the parasympathetic nervous system and not the sympathetic nervous system, which is responsible for triggering the adrenalin that provokes strong anxiety responses.

Many forms of relaxation techniques, such as meditating on Scripture or using imagery, help switch our minds off from anxiety. We can also relax just by doing something that we enjoy, such as these options suggested by delegates at a recent conference:

- Taking a warm bath
- Fly-fishing
- Walking
- Relaxing while listening to music
- Playing an instrument
- Reading
- Writing
- Gardening
- Playing scrabble
- Praying
- Laughing
- Taking time to relax and do nothing else
- Having a cup of tea with a friend.

RELAXATION EXERCISES

Relaxation is a skill, and to acquire it we need to practise it regularly – perhaps daily for a month until the feeling of relaxation becomes familiar to us. The ideal setting for any relaxation exercise is somewhere without distractions, such as sitting or lying down in a quiet room.

One excellent relaxation technique used by counsellors is known as 'progressive muscular relaxation', first developed by an American psychologist, Jacobson, in 1938, and later refined by a general practitioner, Wolpe, and a psychologist, Lazarus, in 1966. It consists of tensing different muscle groups for about six seconds, and then relaxing them for a longer period. This very simple relaxation exercise is often called 'tensing and relaxing' and concentrates on four areas: the face and neck; shoulders and arms; chest, stomach and lower back; and hips, thighs and legs.

TENSING AND RELAXING EXERCISE

Begin as in the breathing exercise with feet slightly apart, eyes looking down or closed, as you again feel the chair take your weight, and rid yourself of intrusive thoughts. Focus on your breathing again, and try to make your out-breath two counts longer than your in-breath.

Now focus on your right hand. Squeeze it tightly into a fist, clenching it tighter and tighter, and be aware of the tension as you do so. Hold for six seconds. Then let the tension go and relax your fingers, letting them go loose for about ten seconds. Repeat.

Now flex your right elbow, tensing your arm and forcing your right knuckle into your right shoulder. Hold this tense position for six seconds, then let your arm go floppy, totally relaxed, and notice the difference. Repeat. Now repeat this with your left hand and arm, then pull your shoulders up to your ears, tense them tightly, and then relax once more.

Continue relaxing other parts of the body in the same way, working upwards via your neck and facial muscles, then downwards using your stomach muscles and buttock muscles, and continuing through your hips, thighs, legs and ankles and lastly by curling up your toes. It may be helpful to think of the words 'calm' or 'peace' each time you breathe out and relax your muscles. Having done this, if you are aware that a particular part of your body still feels tense, repeat the tensing and relaxing exercise for those muscles.

Once your body is relaxed, picture a place that feels very safe to you – a garden, a room, or a favourite part of the countryside – and then ask Jesus to walk with you there. Is He saying anything to you or are you just relaxing in His company? Soak up the peaceful atmosphere and when you are ready, open your eyes and stretch out. This exercise is now complete. You may also like to try the alternative relaxation exercise in Appendix 2.

PHYSICAL EXERCISE
Another way to deal with the physical aspect of anxiety is to combat it with vigorous physical exercise such as walking, jogging, squash or football. Studies show that aerobic physical exercise is not only healthy, but also can reduce muscle tension and relieve frustration.

Anxiety and unhelpful thoughts: psychological change

SKILLS TO REDUCE WORRYING THOUGHTS
Very often it is the views and opinions we hold that cause us anxiety, and accordingly we may have to work on changing our thought life. The two main ways which have proved effective in breaking the cycle of worry are challenging and replacing unhelpful thoughts, and distraction.

1. Challenging unhelpful thoughts

A useful tool to help us challenge our irrational and unhelpful thoughts is the 'A-W-A-R-E' skill, which helps us to look at our anxiety more objectively.

THE 'A-W-A-R-E' SKILL

Step 1: Acknowledge and accept your anxiety

The more people fight anxiety, the more difficult it is to get rid of the anxious feelings. A more constructive approach is to accept the anxiety and work with it. One way is to imagine the anxiety as a shape or even an animal, making it easier to work on the problem as the sufferer can then look at their anxiety more objectively.

Step 2: Watch your anxiety

It can be very helpful to take on the role of a curious observer, monitoring the anxiety's intensity and noting when it peaks and subsides, rating it on a scale from one to ten. Remember you are not your anxiety. Be in the anxiety state, but not of it.

Once the anxiety has been assessed, work towards bringing the level down. This is a far more realistic target than expecting the anxiety to totally disappear, as setting out with a fixed, concrete goal to eradicate the anxiety will often bring even more anxiety and guilt if the goal is not reached!

Step 3: Act with your anxiety

As far as possible, keep behaving normally and aim to do what you set out to do. Breathe normally in a relaxed way, and stay with the anxiety rather than running away. This will help to de-condition the anxiety – the reversal of previous conditioning of a behaviour, especially as a treatment for phobic and other anxiety disorders.

Step 4: Replace your unhelpful thoughts

Learn to challenge unhelpful thinking by asking questions such as:
- What evidence do I have to support my thoughts?
- What evidence do I have against them?
- What alternative views are there?
- How would this be regarded from a Christian perspective?
- What effect does my thinking have on what I do?
- Is this helpful for my long-term goal?

Step 5: Expect to improve and overcome anxiety

Expect the anxiety to get better because it will get better. Although it may not be totally overcome, it can be lessened so that it is manageable. Recognise that what you fear may never happen, and reinforce your progress with positive statements, eg *Learning new skills will help me to effectively handle my anxiety, and it will get less.*

Activity

Write each unhelpful thought down on one side of a piece of paper, and then write a true helpful thought opposite which either challenges the original idea or gives an alternative way of looking at the situation. For example:

Worrying thoughts and images	**Alternative thoughts and views**
I'll never beat this anxiety.	Just take one day at a time. There are lots of things I can do to help myself.
I may have a panic attack and faint.	I've never fainted before. If I control my breathing I will be fine.
I can't face my boss – she's so critical.	Avoiding situations just makes things worse. I am going to learn to speak up for myself, and let her know how I feel. I am going to be assertive in this situation.

Activity

MAKING A THOUGHT RECORD

A thought record teaches us how to identify the link between anxiety and thoughts, and helps us learn how to test and evaluate these thoughts in order to change them. Look at the sample thought record page illustrated (pp84-5), and then return to the anxiety-provoking situation that you used when filling in the Waverley Integrative Framework or alternative anxiety model earlier. Now use this situation as a focus to record your thought responses in your own thought record (a blank thought record page can be found in Appendix 3). Note the triggering event, the intensity of your anxiety, and your irrational self-talk. Now challenge the thoughts by looking at them objectively, based on the evidence you have, and then write in a new, more balanced, rational thought. Say the new self-talk out loud to reinforce the positive thoughts and help your anxiety.

Thought record
(read across both pages)

TRIGGER	MOOD	SELF-TALK/IMAGES
Who? **What?** **When?** **Where?**	**Describe your feelings in one word. Now rate the intensity of your mood (0–10).**	**What was going through your mind just before you started to feel this way? What images or memories come to mind?**
Exams	Anxiety (10)	What if I don't pass? I will be a failure. If I fail it will be awful because then I won't get a promotion.
Friday afternoon Out shopping and about to go up in a lift	Panic (9) Anxiety (10)	I am having palpitations and feel faint. I am having a heart attack. I am going to embarrass myself. Image: Lying on the floor unconscious with people laughing at me.

EVIDENCE	NEW SELF-TALK	RE-RATE MOOD
What factual evidence supports this thought? What factual evidence doesn't support this thought?	**Write an alternative and/or balanced thought.** Write an alternative view of the situation that is consistent with the evidence.	**Re-rate the intensity of your feelings. Hopefully it will have become lower.**
It's the firm's policy that I won't get a promotion if I fail. I have a 100% pass rate with all my exams. God doesn't see me as a failure.	I am very unlikely to fail. If I do, that doesn't mean I am a failure. My best is good enough. God sees me as a person of infinite worth whether I fail or not. (Isa. 43:4) If I don't get a promotion, God still has a plan for my life. (Eph. 1:11–12)	Anxiety (6–7)
A rapid heartbeat doesn't mean I am having a heart attack. Feeling faint with palpitations is all part of anxiety. I have never fainted or had anything wrong with my heart. I have seen a person faint, and nobody laughed. Everyone was helpful and sympathetic.	My doctor reassured me that palpitations are not necessarily dangerous. He said they are more likely to be a symptom of anxiety. In all likelihood my heart will return to normal in a few minutes. I can use the skills I have learnt to manage my anxiety and reduce the symptoms. I have never fainted before, but if I do, people are more likely to be helpful and sympathetic than laugh at me. With God's help I am learning how to overcome anxiety. (Isa. 41:10; Phil. 4:13)	Panic (5) Anxiety (5)

Finding alternative ways of thinking

Although speaking the truth to ourselves is a helpful way of coping with worrying thoughts, not all anxiety sufferers find this easy. An alternative approach can be to ask questions that encourage a logical rather than an emotional response such as, *Are there any reasons for you having worrying thoughts? What is the evidence for what you fear?* The reason for this is that the emotional seat of the brain is mainly in the part called the limbic system, whereas the logical part of the brain is the cerebral cortex. These two parts of the brain do not generally work concurrently, so if you can engage the cerebral cortex, your emotions are likely to lessen because the limbic system will become disengaged.

Another helpful tool that counsellors use in encouraging an objective view is to ask the sufferer what they would say to someone else in the same situation, and then suggest that they take their own advice!

Another way to help people explore their anxiety is by asking the following questions: *What is the worst thing that can happen? What is the best thing that can happen? What is likely to happen? If the worst scenario were to happen, what measures could you put in place to cope?* Questions like these really help people face their anxiety.

> Mel was living in a real anxiety state caused by worry about what she would do if her elderly mother died, although there was no actual evidence to suggest that this would happen in the immediate future. In counselling, Mel was encouraged to face the issue head on with the direct question, 'How would you cope if your mother died?'
>
> As Mel and her counsellor explored answers to this question together, Mel considered various options: *If she died, I could do this, or I could do that* and, as a result, her

> anxiety levels dramatically decreased because she now had a plan of action.

Activity

Replace these worrying thoughts with alternative, balanced thoughts that challenge the anxiety expressed:

Dani is late for our meeting. Her car might have crashed and she may be injured.

_____

I am beginning to sweat and feel sick. I will have to dash to the toilet and that will embarrass me.

_____

I'm anxious that I cannot cope by myself because my husband has left me.

_____

Now make up some examples of your own:

_____
_____
_____
_____

2. Distraction

Distraction is a simple but very effective way to cope with unhelpful thoughts, and can even have a fun element. One option you might like is mental games – engaging your mind in activities such as mental arithmetic, reciting poetry or Scripture, crosswords or simply counting backwards from one hundred in threes, (ninety-seven, ninety-four, ninety-one etc).

Another helpful alternative is to focus on the outside world to distract you, perhaps by listening to a conversation, looking at what colours people are wearing or listing all the things you can hear, see or touch.

We can also engage in the biblical approach to distraction by fixing our gaze upon God.

> 'If you value the approval of God, fix your minds on the things which are holy and right and pure and beautiful and good'
> PHIL. 4:8, PHILLIPS.

Distraction works because it allows you to focus your attention on something other than the unhelpful thoughts. It is not really possible to force yourself not to think about something: the minute you tell yourself not to think about something, you are thinking about it! Distraction, however, makes you direct your attention away from what is making you worried or anxious and onto something else. As you are no longer focused on the unhelpful thoughts, your anxiety is likely to reduce.

When Chris's daughter was ill, anxious thoughts such as *What if this happens? What if that happens?* kept waking Chris up in the middle of the night so that she felt absolutely worn out. To cope with this anxiety Chris learned to take a favourite worship song – 'All hail the Lamb, enthroned on high'[2]– and sing it inwardly whenever her thoughts were running rampant in the middle of the night. Sometimes she would have to do this a number of times before the anxiety subsided but, over time, the whole thing got easier as Chris worshipped instead of worrying.

After about a year, although Chris's situation hadn't changed and her daughter was still ill, her anxiety levels had dramatically decreased as she found herself waking in the middle of the night with the words of the song already on her mind.

> Dean was very anxious about travelling on trains. He could just about get to the station, but was not able to actually get on the train. It was agreed with his counsellor that, armed with his newly learned skills of breathing and distraction, he would board the train and travel just one stop up the line. When standing on the platform Dean looked across to the opposite platform and performed a number of distracting counting tasks. *How many people are wearing red coats? How many black? How many people are wearing glasses? How many are wearing jeans?* Dean found that because his thoughts were occupied by the distraction of looking out for all these things, the feelings of anxiety did not arise. He is now able to get on the train and, having achieved success once, travels on the train without a problem.

The use of imagery techniques can be very powerful.

> 'Those of steadfast mind you keep in peace– in peace because they trust in you'
>
> ISA. 26:3, NRSV.

For instance, when an image associated with anxiety comes up, learn to replace it with an image of God as a strong tower (eg Psa. 61:3) or as the Rock on which you stand (Psa. 40:2). Alternatively, imagine comforting homely images like being wrapped in a warm blanket, or try simple physical distractions such as going for a walk or behavioural activities such as seeing friends.

Meditation quietens your mind and brings a feeling of peace, while another useful tool is the 'traffic lights' distraction technique for stopping unhelpful thought processes. As soon as you start saying negative statements about yourself – *I'm no good. I'm a failure. This is terrible* – mentally picture a red traffic light: *Stop! Red traffic light!* and say to yourself, *I'm not going down that road.* At this point think of new helpful thoughts and visualise the traffic light turning green, allowing you to move off down the road of your new thoughts.

> Leon was having so many anxious thoughts relating to his work that his physical symptoms made it difficult for him to function properly. He used the 'Stop! Red traffic light!' skill to very good effect as he recognised he could choose to take control over stopping his thoughts. His physiological symptoms dramatically reduced, and he was soon able to concentrate again at work and improve his performance.

You can also distract yourself from anxious thoughts by the use of a bridging object. This is an object that represents security to you, perhaps associated with happy memories, eg a favourite teddy or a family photograph. It works by helping bridge from the anxiety-provoking 'here and now' to something that felt safe in the past or a specific memory that evokes good feelings. This is particularly useful for people who have suffered abuse as it helps to provide an alternative focus for their anxious thoughts.

Anxiety and our behaviour: changing behavioural maintaining cycles

Once we understand what is happening when we feel anxious, the next stage is to overcome patterns of avoidance. It can be helpful to draw up a list of all the things you have been avoiding, or currently find difficult to achieve.

A typical list may be:

- Avoiding public transport
- Letting people take advantage of you
- Avoiding being assertive with the boss
- Constantly saying 'No' to social invitations.

BREAKING ANXIETY DOWN INTO MANAGEABLE STAGES

To change anxious behaviour patterns it is important to break the behaviour down into manageable stages, ie into small achievable goals. The goals being small and achievable is important: life can be very difficult and if you try to do too much too quickly, you may be setting yourself up to fail. It is important to go slowly when you are changing anxious behaviour patterns. Consider the following example: if the problem is driving a car around town and a person's goal is to be able to park the car in order to go shopping, we can break it down into several steps as in the following ladder diagram. This represents a 'hierarchy of fear' where the thought of getting to the car park provokes the highest level of anxiety.

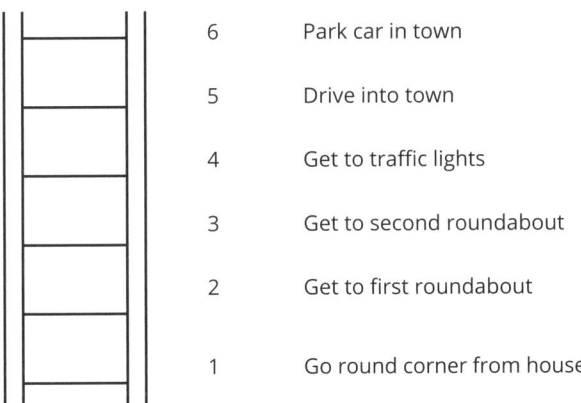

Starting from the bottom the person systematically faces up to the feared situation step by step but, just like climbing a ladder, it is important to feel comfortable with each stage before progressing further. Therefore, each task is performed several times to increase confidence levels, and the sufferer may also find it helpful to score units of anxiety to help monitor their progress.

If the anxiety fails to reduce, or the person has problems facing the feared situation, the rungs on their ladder may be too far apart, and additional steps should be included to break the situation down still further.

Working with the anxiety through gradual exposure, setting small achievable goals, and giving the sufferer tools and skills (eg breathing, relaxing, distraction, helpful thoughts) helps reduce anxiety, and practising each stage until the anxiety is manageable will see real results. Using this graded behavioural technique helps overcome fears and regain lost confidence.

> Ana had had a panic attack in a particular university lecture theatre and subsequently missed lectures there as she was afraid to go back again. She was then worried that this would cause her problems with the work for her degree. She talked about the situation with her counsellor and they planned going to the lecture theatre together and walking past it, which they did a few times. When Ana was ready, they went into the lecture theatre together and also did this a few times. They then planned for Ana to visit the lecture theatre on her own when it was empty, which she did several times until she felt able to go back to lectures there again. She subsequently had no more panic attacks in that lecture theatre.

Activity

Experiment with this behavioural activity and see if it is helpful. Make a 'worry box' by finding a box or tin with a lid. Write your worries down on pieces of paper, put them into the container, and don't look at them again until the following week when you may find, like Arthur below, that your worry has ceased to be a problem.

> Arthur decided to do all his worrying on one day each week. He chose Mondays. When anything happened that gave him anxiety, he would write it down and put it in his worry box and forget about it until the next Monday. The interesting thing was that on the following Monday when he opened his worry box he found that most of the things that had worried him during the past six days had been settled.

Anxiety and our spiritual life: becoming more dependent upon God

> Said the robin to the sparrow:
> 'I should really like to know
> Why these anxious human beings
> Rush about and worry so.'
>
> Said the sparrow to the robin:
> 'Friend, I think that it must be
> That they have no heavenly Father
> Such as cares for you and me.'
> **ELIZABETH CHENEY (1859)** [3]

It can be very difficult as a Christian when we suffer with intense anxiety because we frequently hear the message that Christians are supposed to feel full of joy and peace! However, the truth is that we are all on a journey of deepening our faith, and we all struggle in different ways.

For those who are anxious, the very last thing they need is for other Christians to heap guilt on them by saying things like, *Well, you should trust God in that.* Of course the anxious Christian wants to trust God, but it is a battle.

Chris once came across a quote that really helped her in the times when she found it hard to keep her head above water: 'Those that struggle well are mature Christians.' Just because you struggle does not disqualify you in the Christian life – in fact, struggle is often a time of real growth for us as, when we are surrounded with anxieties, we learn to look more to God for help, recognising our weakness and becoming more dependent on Him.

LEARNING TO TRUST GOD WHEN LIFE SEEMS UNCERTAIN

When we are beset by anxiety God can meet us in our need, but to reach that place of trust in Him we must pass through several key stages: A, B, C and D.

A – Admit your anxiety to God
God can only help us when we admit we have a problem and need His help. Follow David's example in Psalm 142, and be totally honest about how you really feel.

B – Believe that God hears you and is in control
One of the great truths of the Bible is that God is able to guide His people in every circumstance. We read in 2 Corinthians 5:7 that 'we live by faith, not by sight', and that means that we can trust God in the difficult times as well as the good times, knowing that He is in ultimate control of our life.

What do I trust God for? Chris asked herself that question many times when she was experiencing the pain of her daughter's illness. She obviously hoped that God would heal her daughter, but she knew that He might not do that.

So what could Chris trust God for? She trusted Him to be with her in the situation. Just like a trusting child, she could put her hand in her Father's hand, knowing they were walking the path together. She trusted that He loved her, recognising how precious she was to God because He had sent Jesus to die for her, and that He was her living hope.

Feelings are deceptive and will let us down; faith is not based on feelings, but on our knowledge of God's character. God is the one certain factor in our uncertainty. For Chris, placing her trust in such a faithful God meant that she knew He would help her to cope.

C – Consider
Consider what you can do about a situation. Think about the things that you can change and those that you can't. Once you have had this phase of considering then you can move on to the next step and take action.

Be aware that there may be some people who will try to tell you that anxiety is a sin and that you shouldn't be anxious because of verses such as Philippians 4:6 which tells us not to be anxious (NIV) or worry (NRSV) about anything. However, if we look at other verses about anxiety such as 1 Peter 5:7 we are simply encouraged to cast our anxieties onto Him. It is important not to allow yourself to be condemned because you experience anxiety, and to know that God is with you in it.

D – Do
You can go on to change the things that you can change and this may help your anxiety reduce. You can also replace some of the unhelpful thoughts that having anxiety can give you with truths from God's Word. Use helpful techniques like imagery, and especially words of Scripture which can become anchors to stop people slipping into despair. Be like David in the cave where, although he

felt utterly distraught and poured out his anxious feelings ('I cry aloud to the Lord; I lift up my voice to the Lord for mercy. I pour out before him my complaint'), he held on to the anchoring fact, 'You are my refuge' (Psa. 142:5). David acknowledged his feelings with total honesty, but then stopped the free fall as he confessed the truth.

Activity
Think of some Bible verses and Bible stories that could be used to help someone with anxiety.

_____
_____

> Zofia could not rest because she was constantly cleaning to try and keep her house absolutely immaculate. She would work for hours scrubbing and polishing, from very early in the morning to very late at night, driven by her need to make the house absolutely spotless. Looking back to her childhood, Zofia realised that she was trying to be a perfect wife because her father had left her mother, saying that she didn't know how to keep a proper home, and she felt anxious that her husband would leave her if she did not keep the house gleaming: *I must have a perfect house.*
>
> Once she recognised this underlying fear, Zofia then chose to do something about it, and worked towards gradually reducing the amount of housework she did each day. Finally, she was able to find time to do things that she actually enjoyed, like meeting up with friends for coffee or going swimming. Zofia said that the main thing was that she realised she did not have to have an immaculate house, and that her husband and God loved her just the same.

Activity

> Cast all your anxiety on him because he cares for you.
> **1 PETER 5:7**

In his research on the effects of classical music on stress, Eric Whitacre found that stress levels were proven to be reduced through listening to or singing classical music.[4]

You may not like classical music but the research found that when professionals sang in a low-stress rehearsal atmosphere, levels of cortisol and cortisone (the stress hormones that feed into anxiety) went down. This means that anxiety would be reduced. You may want to try singing along to worship songs as this should achieve the same effect. The important thing is that you do actually sing out loud and not just listen or sing quietly. The singing will help with the hormone reduction and the truths contained in the worship songs will be giving your mind accurate information rather than the unhelpful thoughts your anxiety might be giving you.

Reflection

'I have learned to be content whatever the circumstances', wrote the apostle Paul (Phil. 4:11). That doesn't just mean when our circumstances are going well, when the sun is shining on us and we feel good about everything, but also when we find ourselves besieged by difficulties and when we are attacked by fears on all sides. Read Philippians 4, noting verses 6 and 7. Read it again slowly, out loud. Give God your anxiety; let Him take the weight from you. Picture it rolling from your shoulders as you stand in God's presence, like Christian's burden in *The Pilgrim's Progress*.[5] Ask for God's peace to fill you from the tips of your toes to the top of your head, the same contentment 'whatever the circumstances' that Paul had.

Drop thy still dews of quietness.
Till all our striving cease;
Take from our souls the strain and stress,
And let our ordered lives confess
The beauty of thy peace.[6]
J.G. WHITTIER

Prayer

I know that Your love surrounds me every single moment of every single day, Lord. Thank You so much that You understand my humanity, and the times when I become anxious. Help me to remember in those moments that You are my refuge and my security. Since I have known You, it has changed my life for ever – I cannot live without You, nor would I want to. Help me not to keep trying to do things my own way, but to follow You with my whole heart. Thank You that life with You is an adventure. I am looking forward to all that You have in store for me, and of walking beside You with my hand in Yours. Amen.

> May the God of hope fill you with all joy and peace as you trust in him…
> **ROMANS 15:13**

Appendices

Appendix 1:

Helping an anxiety sufferer

When coming alongside someone with anxiety, it can be helpful to make an outline of what is happening to them, and use this as a springboard to work on practical strategies to move them forward, eg *What tools and skills may be helpful for their anxious thoughts? What strategy may be helpful for their behaviour? How can they be helped to grow spiritually?*

1. What sort of anxiety is the person suffering with?

___

2. How is their anxiety affecting the different areas of their life?

Physical

___

Mental

___

Behavioural

___

Spiritual

___

3. Where might you start to help them?

_____
_____

4. What tools and skills would you use to help each area of their life? (Choose one skill or tool for each area)

Physical

_____

Mental

_____

Behavioural

_____

Spiritual

_____

Appendix 2:

Alternative relaxation exercise

Sit or lie as comfortably as possible, and close your eyes.
(If during this exercise you experience unusual sensations such as tingling or light-headedness, this is quite normal. If you open your eyes these sensations will go away, and as you carry on with the exercise they will disappear.)

Become aware of your breathing.
Keeping your eyelids closed, screw your eyes up tightly, and then

relax them.
Notice the tiredness in those muscles around your eyes. Let the warmth of God's healing light relax those muscles further.
Let that feeling of warmth travel to every part of your face, jaw, tongue and neck.
Relax and bathe in God's healing light.
Concentrate on your breathing.

Then let the healing warmth travel slowly down through every part of your body, stopping regularly to pause and concentrate on your breathing.

Allow the healing warmth to relax your shoulders, to travel down your right arm, down through the muscles, down to your fingertips. Do the same with the left arm. Let the relaxation travel down to your chest, your back, and down each leg in turn. Pause for a few moments.

Go back and concentrate on any part of the body you would like to relax further.

Now concentrate on your favourite relaxing place (real or imagined). Try and see it in your mind's eye.
Identify the shapes and colours, the sounds and smells. Imagine touching something in this peaceful place.
Is Jesus in this place? Is He saying anything to you? Feel more and more relaxed.

Stay in this place of peace and relaxation until you are ready to return to the room, taking your own time to do this slowly.

Appendix 3:
Extra thought record page for your own use

Thought record

TRIGGER	MOOD	SELF-TALK/IMAGES

EVIDENCE	NEW SELF-TALK	RE-RATE MOOD

Endnotes

CHAPTER 1
1. Somers Roche, cited in V. Ritterbusch, *Reframe Your Viewpoints* (Orlando FL: Life Changes Publishing House, 2021).
2. *Compact Oxford English Dictionary* (Oxford: Oxford University Press, 1996).
3. *Collins English Dictionary* (London: Collins, 1976).
4. Plante & Sherman, *Faith & Health, Psychological Perspectives* (New York: Guilford Press, 2001).

CHAPTER 2
1. C.S. Lewis, *Letters to Malcolm: Chiefly on Prayer* (London: William Collins, 1964).

CHAPTER 3
1. C.S. Lewis, *Letters to Malcolm: Chiefly on Prayer* (London: Collins, 1964, published posthumously).

CHAPTER 4
1. Corrie Ten Boom, *Clippings from My Notebook* (T. Nelson, 1982).
2. *Diagnostic and Statistical Manual of Mental Disorders*, Fourth Edition. Primary Care Version (USA: American Psychiatric Association, 1995).
3. Yackel, K., Schwarz, L. A., Kam, K. Sorokin, J. M., Feldman, J. L., Luo, L. & Krasnow, M. A. (2017) Breathing control center neurons that promote arousal in mice, Science, 355 (6332), 1411-1415.
4. NHS Inform. [Online] Available at: nhsinform.scot/illnesses-and-conditions/mental-health/phobias. (Accessed 4/1/2023).

CHAPTER 5
1. Cited in *The 7 Habits of Highly Effective People* by S. R. Covey
2. Dave Bilbrough © 1987 Kingsway's Thankyou Music.
3. Quoted in J. John and Mark Stibbe, *A Box of Delights,* (London: Monarch Books, 2001)
4. Gramophone. (2015) New scientific study shows that singing and attending classical music concerts physically reduces stress. [Online]. Available at: gramophone.co.uk/classical-music-news/article/new-scientific-study-shows-that-singing-and-attending-classical-music-concerts-physically-reduces-stress. (Accessed 4/1/2023).
5. John Bunyan, *The Pilgrim's Progress* (Oxford: Oxford World's Classics: Oxford University Press, 2003).
6. J.G. Whittier 1807–92.

Further reading

Baker R., *Understanding Panic Attacks and Overcoming Fear* (Oxford: Lion Publishing, 1995).

Beck A.T., *Anxiety Disorders and Phobias: A Cognitive Perspective* (New York: Basic Books, 1985).

Benson H., *Beyond the Relaxation Response* (New York: Times Books, 1984).

Gittelman R., *Anxiety Disorders of Childhood* (New York: Guilford Press, 1986).

Kennerley Helen, *Overcoming Anxiety: A self-help guide using Cognitive Behaviour Techniques* (London: Constable and Robinson, 1997).

Last C.G. and Hersen M., *Handbook of Anxiety Disorders* (New York: Pergamon Press, 1987).

Lawson Michael, *Facing Anxiety and Stress* (London: Hodder & Stoughton, 1986).

Mitchell R., *Phobias* (Harmondsworth: Penguin Books, 1982).

Sharpe Robert, *Self-help for your Anxiety* (London: Souvenir Press, 1997).

Spielberger C., *Understanding Stress and Anxiety* (New York: Harper & Row, 1979).

Wilson R.R., *Don't Panic: Taking Control of Anxiety Attacks* (London: HarperCollins, 1986).

WAVERLEY ABBEY COLLEGE

Develop your gifts • Be equipped • Make a difference

Equipping people to be the positive impact on society through courses in:

- **Counselling**
- **Spiritual Formation**
- **Contemporary courses in Chaplaincy, Discipleship and Church Ministry**

waverleyabbeycollege.ac.uk

A hub of spiritual encounter, Christian education, innovative enterprise and community engagement.

Waverley Abbey Trust is a ministry, equipping you to love God, love your neighbour and love yourself.

Through our portfolio of courses and resources, you can learn to be the difference in society.

Find out more today.

waverleyabbeytrust.org